Tales of Tinderella

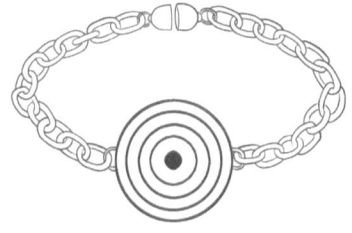

JULIE OKELY & SIMONE HAMILTON

Copyright © 2019 by **Julie Okely & Simone Hamilton**

All rights reserved. No part of this publication may be reproduced, distributed or transmitted in any form or by any means, without prior written permission.

Karen Mc Dermott
Perth, WA
www.karenmcdermott.com.au

Publisher's Note: This is a work of fiction. Names, characters, places, and incidents are a product of the author's imagination. Locales and public names are sometimes used for atmospheric purposes. Any resemblance to actual people, living or dead, or to businesses, companies, events, institutions, or locales is completely coincidental.

Cover design: Debrja Day
Typesetting: Chelsea Wilcox
Editor: Gaëtane Burkolter AE
Proofreader: Dannielle Line

Julie Okely & Simone Hamilton/ Tales of Tinderella.
ISBN 978-0-6485891-0-5 (sc)
ISBN 978-0-6485891-1-2 (e)

Disclaimer: This is a work of fiction. Names, characters, businesses, places, events and incidents are either the products of the author's imagination or used in a fictitious manner. Any resemblance to actual persons, living or dead, or actual events is purely coincidental.

To our children, Taylah, Ayden, Josh and Hannah,
who deserve the loving relationships we want for them.

Rising above my Flames

Rising above sorrow's flames
Seeing the phoenix of my spirit
Come to the stars
My heart is open and full
The grey is gone, and the sky is blue
Crystal sparkling flashes of gold and true
Holding hands and feeling the dream
My heart is yours and you hold it
Fragile and fractured never again

New beginnings for me
Walking as one
Never alone
Finally, complete
You are my hero
Life I embrace
With you
I belong

Julie Okely

Acknowledgements

Writing about such a diverse range of dating stories in this digital age has proven to be an enlightening experience. Who would have thought you could become the president of your very own dating agency? All the time picking and choosing amongst those who could be your next potential partner... or not!

In our research, we went to the experts, who included all of our female contacts, friends and family members. We wanted to hear everything—every story, every situation and every urban legend.

We organized several 'ladies only' events, and we laughed and cried through the many stories of lust, failure and sizzle. Our research provided a chance for us to drink many coffees, sip some lovely Australian wines and giggle, while sharing stories with this gorgeous group of gals. From those stories, we could base our chapters on real-life events and turn them from verbal stories into the printed word and boom! Tinderella was born.

This would not have been such an exciting journey if it were not for these get-togethers with our case study gals. So, to these beautiful women, we say THANK YOU.

We brought many of these shared stories to life throughout *Tales of Tinderella* for you, our loyal readers. By sharing Tinderella's experiences during her online dating journey, we hope to provide the right balance of advice, support and encouragement to other women also seeking 'the One'—or just a newfound sense of self.

At the time of writing this, I think about us, the authors. We are both single mothers, and our lives revolve around the needs of our busy children. Endless days that intertwine with the demands of work, friendships, family near and far, along with maintaining our homes, cuddling our puppies and enjoying life!

It is with the deepest of love we pay tribute to and thank our children (Julie: Taylah and Ayden; and Simone: Josh and Hannah) for their understanding, patience and encouragement. It was wonderful to see the cheerleader come out in them as they watched their mums complete this exciting, and at times all-consuming adventure. Well done, gorgeous kids, on stepping up and sharing the load, which helped us to keep tapping away on our laptops, bringing Tinderella to life!

Thank you to our fabulous editor, Gaëtane Burkolter, for keeping us both focused on writing our best book. You helped to ensure that we never lost sight of our 'why'—the deep desire to help women feel supported in their journey for love. Your encouragement and advice to us both throughout this process meant the world to us.

Many thanks also to our fabulous publisher, Karen McDermott. Karen, thank you for taking us on as clients—even before our book was finished! We are so grateful to you for believing in us and our project. Your kind, patient encouragement and support in bringing our book to print allowed us to fulfil a lifelong dream.

We would not be who we are today without the love and support from our families and beautiful friends. This dream would not be possible without your desire to hear Tinderella's stories and the faith you invested in us to deliver on writing this book. We are both so very blessed to have so many amazing people in our lives and as much as we would love to mention everyone here; it isn't possible. We promise to take great joy in thanking you all individually, in our own way.

We were blessed to have had the chance to write our book in the most beautiful locations, which included some spectacular water views, beautiful nature, fabulous local restaurants, awesome pubs… and the odd sexy body walking past—spotted by Tinderella, of course!

Thank you, Tinderella, too—for giving us a new love of pinot gris, champagne, fashion and good times!

And finally, thank you to all of our wonderful readers and Tinderella supporters. Without you, where would Tinderella be?

To our romantics, thank you for believing that you are indeed worthy of love and a loving relationship.

To our non-believers, we ask that you please embrace the incredible opportunities for growth and learning along the way and live the best life you can.

Our goal in writing this book was to entertain, educate and enlighten women just like ourselves, who are searching for life, love and happiness. Wherever you are on your journey, we embrace your decision to start or to continue your search for what you need, and we acknowledge your commitment to the process. Please, always remember everything in life is a lesson, and the journey is just as important as the destination.

Julie Okely

Simone Hamilton

Foreword

By Simone Hamilton, Behavioural Change Specialist

Dating was certainly different twenty to thirty years ago—yes, last century, when many of us first experienced the dating scene after leaving high school. We were young, and most of us were naïve in our early search for a life partner. We generally enjoyed meeting people through our social circles at university or work, church, barbeques, parties and clubs. Perhaps we even had well-meaning friends who loved matchmaking us with their own friends. Essentially, we met people *through other people*.

Today, it seems to be increasingly difficult to meet people with whom to explore the possibility of establishing solid and meaningful personable relationships. Finding a soul mate even more so. We tend to rely on social media platforms such as Facebook and WhatsApp to connect and stay in touch with friends, rather than doing this face-to-face. You probably have more conversations via SMS than face-to-face. The United Nations Telecommunications statistics report that 8.2 billion SMS messages were sent every day worldwide during 2016[1]. As a result, the way we communicate with people and develop and foster relationships with others is changing. Traditional options to meet people still exist, such as joining a club, interest group or sports team, or attending social gatherings with a friend, but more and more people are turning to online dating apps to meet potential partners.

---

[1] Measuring The Information Society Report 2018, International Telecommunication Union (ITU), 2018, https://www.itu.int/en/ITU-D/Statistics/Documents/publications/misr2018/MISR2018-ES-PDF-E.pdf

When we are fortunate enough to find someone who we want to spend the rest of our lives with, we enter that lifelong relationship thinking 'life' really means 'for life'. We enjoy the good times and we work hard during the challenging times. Sadly, for many, these partnerships that held so much promise don't last. Statistics indicate that 30% of first-time marriages end in divorce[2].

When we commit to a lifelong relationship, we commonly shun that figure—certain in the belief we will be in the other two-thirds.

Yet there are an increasing number of women who find themselves single after 20-plus years of marriage. In my practice, I see many people who are struggling after the breakdown of a relationship and fearful about living a life on their own. Some vow never to be in a relationship again, while others still hold out hope. One of my clients is sixty-three years old. She came to me for help to 'have a good life now', having finally had the courage to leave her abusive husband after forty years of marriage.

I, too, am a woman of our times; a middle-aged, twice-divorced soul mate searcher. I've smiled inside reading the trials and tribulations of Tinderella, thinking to myself: oh my goodness—this is me! Or, yes—that happened to me too!

So, I am pleased to contribute to this book on two levels—as a behavioural change specialist, and as a woman who has been on a similar journey to Tinderella.

Tales of Tinderella is more than just a light read about dating experiences. It is brimful of insights into human behaviour. Throughout this book, in my role as a relationship coach, I will guide you through the landscape of online dating by shining some light on the human behaviours, personalities, values and sexual inclinations of the men whom Tinderella encounters. This in turn may just benefit you

---

[2] https://www.budgetdirect.com.au/blog/marriage-and-divorce-statistics-australia.html

when meeting new people on your dating journey—perhaps even in your day-to-day life.

It is my hope that by reading this book, it will inspire you to let go of any negative online dating experiences you've had in your past, and to feel empowered to embrace—and enjoy—meeting new and interesting people through online dating. It's actually just as much about your own journey of self-discovery, as it is about your experiences with meeting new people.

Tinderella in this book is you. She is me. She is all the sisterhood who are searching for true love and lifelong partnerships.

Important Disclaimer

Included in this book is the guidance and advice I've drawn from many years of experience as a neuro-linguistic master practitioner, master hypnotherapist, and relationships and human behavioural specialist. During this time, I worked closely with psychologists, psychiatrists and other therapists to jointly manage the needs of mutual clients and provide effective support.

The perspectives I have provided in this book and the discussions we've opened up have created a new platform to explore aspects of online dating. However, the content of this book is not intended to be a substitute for professional medical advice, diagnosis, or treatment.

We recommend that you seek the advice of your physician or other qualified health provider with any questions you may have regarding a medical condition, and for support and advice on matters relating to your mental health.

CONTENTS

Rising above my Flames 5
Acknowledgements 7
Foreword 11
Introduction 17
Sean 19
Don 32
Aaron 46
Jackson 56
Ben 72
Mick 81
Baz 94
Brad 103
James 111
Nigel 123
Joe 138
Gary 147
Steve 161
Sam 177
Lenny 189
Andrew 202
Ron 212
Derrick 222
Ken 234
The Reflection 249
References & Resources 251
About the Authors 255

Introduction

I would never have guessed that I would one day become one of the many women searching for intimacy, love or companionship all over again. But it happened. At forty-four years old, and after over two decades of marriage, divorce became a reality and a new chapter of my life beckoned.

After years of being a wife, mother, homemaker and manager of my own business, now I faced the exciting and daunting status of being 'single'.

I married in my early twenties and had little experience in the art of dating, let alone with anything in today's online landscape. The prospect of getting out there and meeting a new man was a whole different world to navigate. The only way to do it was to dive right in.

A hairdresser by trade, I have enjoyed many years of listening to stories from my clients. As I strode and stumbled my way through this new dating experience, we shared some of our adventures, and they encouraged me to put them to paper.

Tinderella was born, and her tales are here to be shared.

We wrote *Tales of Tinderella* to help you through the rough times of failed relationships, one-night stands and torrid ordeals that can come from putting yourself out there again in the search for love. These shared stories reassure you that you are not alone, and that as a sisterhood we are each travelling on our own individual path to self-discovery.

Tinderella's experiences are based on true stories drawn from that sisterhood, with some embellishment and embroidery, to provide you with a wide-ranging look at the dating scene today. Women have always bonded over stories, teaching and supporting one another through shared experience. Understand that not every story is an actual event lived by the author, but do enjoy this Tinderella's road of discovery and learn from her victories, and her losses.

We have changed all names and pertinent details to protect the innocent... and the guilty.

Each chapter concludes with advice from our behavioural change specialist, Simone Hamilton, who gives her insights into each encounter to help you understand why things happened as they did. She draws out important lessons you can use to protect your own heart, wallet and body. Please absorb what is relevant to you and your own personal story.

Our Tinderella is a sensitive woman with love in her heart and a desire to find her soul mate with whom to share her future. Her openness to possibility is one of her most endearing qualities. I believe there is a little piece of Tinderella in every girl or woman we all know, no matter where you live. I hope that, through her story, you will be motivated to find the courage inside yourself to search for your own True Love. He must be out there!

And so, on with the *Tales of Tinderella*. Sit back and have a read. Enjoy a cup of tea, a glass of wine or just pass the time. The biggest question is:

'Will Tinderella be able to find true love with the right guy, at the right time—when she needs it most?'

As her friend, I hope so.

CHAPTER ONE

Sean

Photography deals exquisitely with appearances, but nothing is what it appears to be.
- Duane Michals

Tinderella was about to take a leap of faith into the unknown. She had decided she wouldn't sit and feel sorry for herself any longer, so she did it. She registered on Tinder.

After the drama and the media reports of Tinder being unpredictable, it took Tinderella from her comfort zone to join, but what was the alternative?

Sure, she had choices.

She could sit at home, eat till she couldn't fit into any of her clothes, drink until she passed out, and become the lady who adopted twenty cats while watching the soaps all day.

But that wasn't the path that would take her to what she wanted. She looked at the positives and thought about what she could do for herself to improve her social life and build her networks and self-esteem. She really wasn't sure whether online dating was the way to do it, but she reminded herself she could easily delete her account if it didn't work out. Tinderella decided to take the risk.

She clicked on 'join through Facebook' and became a registered member.

The Tinder tutorial gave her a good idea of what to do and she began to update her profile pictures. She made sure these were current and included pictures of her size 16 figure. She didn't want any guys coming back to her saying they had expected a skinnier girl or thought her pictures weren't a true likeness.

She added some information about herself, not a lot, just enough to sound cheery and inviting, keeping it very G-rated, with no suggestive pictures. She wanted to meet normal guys who were local and hopefully interested in seeing her more than once.

Tinderella knew the whole dating game had changed since she was last dating twenty-five years before, but she had faith in herself. This was something she had to try.

All set up, she started to look through the potential partners online. She wasn't looking for a relationship—she'd only been separated a few weeks, but she needed companionship. She had needs, and she wanted to discover them.

Tinderella met her ex-husband Peter when she was seventeen and had been married to him for over twenty years. She needed to see if she was attractive to the opposite sex and online dating apps offered the quickest way to find this type of connection. Tinderella had done her research and talked to other women. She'd been very surprised to find many had met their partners on dating sites. With quite a few having had success with this type of dating, it couldn't be all bad.

The men on Tinder were like a smorgasbord of testosterone, and she was feeling a little overwhelmed. But, she sorted through the potentials and was soon flicking the guys that appealed to her to the right.

It wasn't long before she started to get a mutual interest from the other side and was matched for compatibility.

One of her first matches was Sean—a father of two who had been single for five years. He had shared custody of his two young sons, and his profile pictures showed a rugged handsomeness that appealed to Tinderella. It wasn't long before they were in a full conversation through online messaging and began to see they had similar interests. Sean was very witty and had a great sense of humour.

The conversations were engaging, and it wasn't long before she focused solely on him and began to look forward to their daily chats. She was curious to see how they would connect in real life, but at the time he had custody of his children, so it took them a week of online messages and phone calls before they could arrange a time to see each other.

Tinderella had received some good tips from her girlfriend, Eliza, who had been dating for a while.

'You'll know in the first five minutes whether he has potential for an ongoing relationship.'

'Always meet them at a public place—it's easier to get away if needed.'

'And always be at the bar when drinks are purchased. You don't want anyone to slip something into your drink.'

With all that in mind, Tinderella agreed to meet Sean.

Her first Tinder date.

Here she was, a 40-plus, nearly divorced single parent, out on the dating scene. She was stepping into the unknown and she wasn't entirely sure what to expect. Looking back on it later, she really didn't realise how courageous she was being.

One thing she *was* sure of was that she wanted to look fantastic.

She knew what she had to do.

She had to go shopping.

This called for a new outfit and there were plenty of boutiques close to her, so off she went. She found a flattering halter-neck top with little sparkles all over it—it made her feel fantastic.

She'd agreed to meet Sean for drinks, dinner and maybe clubbing after that—this top was black, and styled with just the right amount of sexy, perfect for their planned evening. This was it; this was what she would wear.

Tinderella took her time getting ready, applying her makeup with care and precision. She washed her hair and blow-dried it so it flowed smoothly over her shoulders. It was black, shiny and straight. Perfect.

She wanted to look amazing, so she had chosen her black faux leather pants to wear with her favourite pair of beige heels. The pants clung to her legs and showed off their shape. Yes, she had good legs, and she was going to show them off!

For the final touch, Tinderella added a favourite piece of jewellery for good luck, a beautiful handmade, sterling silver bracelet she had purchased from her travels back into Indigenous community. Tinderella had fallen in love with it because it was so versatile. It had a magnetic clasp and could easily convert to a necklace by tying two ribbons to each end. She could wear it with nearly any outfit. She loved her waterhole bracelet, and it had its own beautiful red box that kept it safe between wears.

Tinderella gave herself a once-over in the mirror. She looked great in this new outfit, and that gave her confidence.

She needed it, too, because she was excited and very nervous at the same time. She had asked Eliza to drop her off at the venue for her date, so she had someone to help steady her nerves a little. She was ready.

After waving goodbye to Eliza, Tinderella checked out the local bar where she had arranged to meet Sean. He had sent her a message to say he would be waiting outside. She could feel her palms beginning to sweat, which didn't happen to her often, only when she was very nervous. She was a little shocked she felt this way tonight—after all, wasn't this what she wanted?

Tinderella walked closer to the bar, and there she saw him.

Sean walked toward her, smiling.

Her heart dropped.

After years of working with the public, Tinderella was proud to say she had an amazing ability to switch on her poker face whenever needed. She needed it.

He looked nothing like his profile pictures.

Tinderella was devastated.

Later, when she described this to her friends, she said, 'I expected to meet Vin Diesel and instead Monty Burns from the

Simpsons was walking toward me.' She may have exaggerated that a little, but she really felt let down.

Tinderella had always endeavoured to treat people with respect, and would never deliberately humiliate someone, so she greeted Sean with a smile, and they walked inside.

Sean was polite and seemed very nice, although she knew from that first moment they were incompatible. Even though they had connected online on an emotional and mental level, she needed to be physically attracted to him, too, and she knew she wasn't. It was disappointing, but she had to follow her feelings. This guy wasn't the one.

They talked for a bit about online dating and the experiences he had been through. Tinderella wasn't the only woman who felt his profile pictures were misleading. He obviously had his reasons for not changing them to be more current, and the more they spoke, the more she learnt about his past and why he was the person sitting in front of her.

Sean's wife had left him five years earlier to begin a relationship with her barista and he was holding a great deal of resentment about the whole situation. Tinderella could feel his pain. It was clear in the way he spoke. He was very bitter and every time he mentioned his wife's name, his eyes would cloud over.

The hurt was too deep for Sean and Tinderella thought perhaps someone had broken him beyond repair. At that moment in time she really felt for this guy and wasn't sure she would want to carry the weight of rejection he was enduring. She truly hoped one day he would find the right girl. And she knew it wasn't her.

They parted ways and Tinderella was deeply shaken. Was this what single life was going to bring to her? Constant disappointment? Loneliness... despair?

She walked into the nearest club and ordered two tequila shots and a gin and tonic—she needed a band-aid. It didn't help. The tears came.

Tinderella felt worthless and alone.

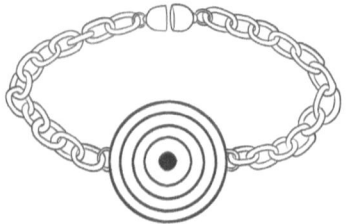

It's Time to Talk... by Simone

DEALING WITH PROFILE PICS AND PHOTOS

People *do* judge a book by its cover. Whether we admit it or not, Profile photos are what initially attracts us to the guys we meet online. Their photos help to make that all-important first impression. Unfortunately, as Tinderella discovered, many people experience a mismatch between who they thought they would meet based on a profile photo and the man they actually meet in person. Sean was clearly not who she thought she would meet—in his looks or his personality.

It is human nature to want to put our best foot forward, so it's not uncommon for people to feel nervous about putting themselves 'out there' for the world to view and pass judgement on. Sometimes this nervousness, combined with a fear of rejection, can lead to a sense of desperation strong enough to drive some to embellish their profile pictures. This is more likely if that person has low self-esteem. In Sean's case, where he hadn't had much dating success for a while, he may have hoped that 'once they meet me, they will like me'. It may even have been a case of him thinking he really 'didn't look that much older/bigger now than I do in my profile photos'.

It is fair to say that women, in particular, are awake to this. We know what we want in our life partners, and an important quality we are looking for is trust and honesty.

Of course, women as well as men can be guilty of not posting honest profile pictures. The key is to be yourself and be proud of who you are and how you look.

Catfishing

A more sinister reason people use misleading photos is because they are catfishing. A 'catfish' is a person who pretends to be someone else online. People use this tactic for deceptive or criminal purposes[3]. For example, a man pretends to be someone else by using a photo that is 'too good to be true' to lure unsuspecting women looking for love[4]. These men play on the assumption that women would feel flattered that a good-looking guy has connected with them. The man's profile description may also be written in a way to elicit emotional responses in women viewers, such as the desire for financial security (the man suggests he is wealthy or owns multiple cars/houses); feelings of sympathy (the man is a widower); or admiration (he is in the armed forces or emergency services).

Note that technology has becomes so sophisticated people can even manipulate video material to create the impression you are seeing a 'live' person in action. Be very wary of anyone who continually fobs you off and avoids meeting in person.

Here are some signs to help you spot someone who is catfishing:

- He avoids meeting in person or over Skype. He may also say he travels a lot with his work to avoid meeting you.
- He quickly wants you to move from chatting within the online dating app, to chatting via SMS, email or Facebook Messenger, giving him direct access to your private information.
- His grammar/spelling isn't great. You may be chatting online with someone from another country who could be catfishing with multiple women at once.

A picture is worth a thousand words

Profile photos portray the visual 'story' of a person and go way beyond just their headshot. We are drawn to a guy's photo as some-

---

[3] https://www.abc.net.au/news/2018-07-26/why-catfish-trick-people-online/10035624

[4] https://www.abc.net.au/news/2019-04-09/lincoln-lewis-fake-catfish-internet-stalker-court-trial/10919538

thing 'catches our eye', or because there's 'just something about him'. When swiping left or right through profile pictures, we are looking for what draws us toward or away from the person on our screens. Our mind filters through the following information in a matter of seconds:
- What are they wearing?
- Who are they with?
- What is their facial expression?
- What are they holding in their hands?
- What is in the background?
- Where are they when the picture was taken?

Tips to choosing your own profile photo

Tinderella carefully considered how she wanted to look in her profile picture and the image of herself that she wanted to portray to men.

Take the time to think about what you want to convey about yourself and how this can be portrayed in a single picture, as well as any additional photos you upload. Be honest with how you portray yourself. Consider the type of person you are hoping to meet—they will be drawn to the person you really are.

Look through photos of yourself on your phone and other social media sites to find photos in which you not only look great, but which are a true indicator of who you are.

Remember, you don't have to be a perfect '10' for these photos. It's only natural to feel slightly nervous about how the opposite sex will perceive you—particularly if you haven't dated for a long time. Again, just be yourself. Embrace who you are and how you look.

If you're feeling a little unsure about yourself, then try this exercise: Look in the mirror, smile, and tell yourself aloud that you are indeed beautiful—the whole you! What an amazing and gorgeous gift you are to a wonderful man who will love you unconditionally.

Profile photo checklist
- Think about how to best portray 'who you are' with your facial expression and in your body language.

- Choose an outfit that is a true reflection of who you are.
- Include your pet in your profile photo if it is important enough in your life to be a consideration in any future relationship.
- Think about what to include in the background of your photo to indicate your interests, your lifestyle and your life passions.
- Your kids may be an important part of your life; however, I suggest that you do not include them in your pictures to ensure their privacy and safety. Note that reputable dating sites will not allow you to include photos of children. You can mention them in your profile description but avoid giving your children's ages if they are under 18.

DEALING WITH FIRST DATE NERVES

Once you've agreed to meet someone for a first date, it is only natural to feel nervous, even more so if it's your very first date on your online dating journey. Many people entering online dating haven't been on a date in years—particularly those who married young or have exited a long-term relationship.

Meeting someone who could potentially become your life partner may make you feel you are 'on show' and this can be daunting. It may bring up feelings of inadequacy or other fears, whether you are normally a confident person.

Here are a few suggestions to help you with those first date nerves:

- Take the pressure off by removing the expectation that the man you are about to date may become your life partner. Look at it for what it is—it's just a date.
- Remind yourself that you are meeting up with this man to determine whether you want to meet him again for a **second** date.
- Remind yourself that you have so much to offer and bring to a relationship. Assume you will impress him. If you need to,

make a list of your best qualities to eliminate any feelings of inadequacy.
- Before you meet him, sit quietly for a few moments and breathe deeply. As you do, visualise yourself on the date. See yourself feeling relaxed, happy and comfortable. Imagine him smiling and hanging off your every word.
- Perhaps have a glass of wine before you leave home, but don't drink too much while you're on your date. You want to have a positive experience, not one you'll regret.
- If you are anxious about what to talk about, be ready with some topics to help keep the conversation flowing. This will also help you feel prepared and 'in control'.
- No matter what happens—remember that you are the one in control and it is your choice whether to see him again.

DEALING WITH PAIN AND PAST HURTS

Sean was not the confident, happy person he portrayed before meeting Tinderella. The wounds from his past are clearly still raw and he couldn't help sharing his pain with her. This is not an uncommon situation to come across when you begin dating, and men see it in the women they meet, too. In fact, it would be quite unusual to come across someone in the online dating world who has not experienced loss, pain, guilt, shame or regret from past relationships

Be wary of taking on someone else's pain. As women, many of us take on the caregiver role and this teaches us to be highly sympathetic towards other people's woes. Be aware, though, that other people's pain can trigger our own underlying hurts, particularly if the shared experience is an acrimonious or hostile divorce. We may even find ourselves in a downward spiral if we spend too much time with a negative new date/partner. If the other person is still suffering from such old pain, it is likely to make them less available to you for a healthy, positive relationship.

Four Stages of the Healing Journey

Everyone's healing journey is different and in my practice I refer to four stages in the healing journey:

Stage 1 – Heartache
Stage 2 – Healing
Stage 3 – Hope
Stage 4 – Happiness

Sean appears to be stuck in the first stage—heartache. He may feel that he is doing okay and is ready for love, even though he clearly isn't. People in the Heartache stage are usually not ready to date and need to spend more time healing. They can achieve this through reflection, personal development, seeking hobbies/interests/experiences that give them joy, or counselling.

Perhaps this is something to consider for yourself if you are still in the early stages of your own healing journey. If you are finding it difficult to move past the heartache stage, a useful first step is to see your doctor for support.

LEARNINGS FROM TINDERELLA AND SEAN

1. Profile pictures are an important indicator of a person's personality, lifestyle and interests, so choose your own carefully. Your profile picture must be a 'truthful' representation of you. Posting an outdated photo that does not portray who you are will only result in disappointment and/or rejection.

2. It's normal to be nervous about going on a first date. There are some things you can do to help you feel relaxed and ready to meet a guy for the first time. Remember, he's likely to be nervous as well.

3. There are lots of hurting people out there. Chances are that many of them are on online dating sites to help them feel better about themselves by jumping into a new relationship to dampen their

pain. Look for signs that may indicate what stage your date is at in their healing journey. You are their date, not their counsellor.

CHAPTER TWO

Don

Human beings, who are almost unique in having the ability to learn from the experience of others, are also remarkable for their apparent disinclination to do so.

— Douglas Adams

After the disaster of her first online date, Tinderella knew she needed more advice. She went back to her friend Eliza, who had been single for the past four years and was a regular on the online dating scene.

'It really doesn't take long to know if he's a good match. Ask your guy key questions to see if you have common ground you can focus on in conversation.'

'Ask them the history of their failed relationships, too.'

'And find out where they live—80kms away isn't a good start.'

'But my number one tip is to see if their profile pictures are current. Men tend to see themselves as they were years earlier, and most of them put up pics from when they were in their prime, but of course age changes them, and they can look so different in real life.'

Tinderella had already been catfished once and didn't want to go through that experience again, but trying to make sure profile pics were recent, staying on top of all these tips … this just sounded too complicated. She felt as if she was interviewing potential dates! Clearly she was years behind in the dating game. It was time to catch up, and she had to do it fast. She needed to get control of what she wanted from this experience and she had to learn this new version of an old game.

Tinderella picked up her iPhone and opened the Tinder app. She wanted to have sex, and for the first time in decades it would be with a new partner—she needed to find a guy to be her ice breaker. She found him and his name was Don.

Don was a plumber and by the look of his pictures, he was still in pretty good shape. She made contact and swiped right. While she waited for a response, Tinderella got on with the business of dressing up for a Saturday night out on the town with her friends. What to wear that suited both clubbing and a first meeting? It had to be funky and modern. Tinderella had an enviable range of clothes in her wardrobe, chosen so she could easily mix and match to suit the occasion.

Tonight, she felt like she needed to wear red. In moments, she had her hands on the piece she would wear. A jumpsuit. It fitted her curves in all the right places and showed just enough cleavage. She could match it back with patent leather stilettos—but which pair? Maybe the silver? Yes, she thought, the silver ones. Her lucky silver waterhole bracelet finished the outfit perfectly. She pulled her hair into a high ponytail. Tinderella blew a kiss to the brunette whose reflection sparkled back at her from the mirror. 'Looking good, sister!'

She was ready for fun.

She would be in the city with her friends, with easy access from most suburbs. The plan to meet Don was in play. Her phone dinged as she put her lipstick into her clutch. Don had responded. After a few exchanges, Tinderella asked him if he wanted to meet with her later that night. He said he'd been at a backyard barbeque, drinking, and probably shouldn't drive.

This was an unanticipated hiccup in the plan.

It wasn't looking good—they couldn't seem to connect on where and when to meet, how she would get there, or if he would get a lift in to the city. But where there is a will, there's a way, and after a few more exchanges they had a plan.

Don said he would stop drinking and meet her in town at midnight. He assured Tinderella that he would be under the legal alcohol limit by then, and okay to drive. She was a woman on a mission and agreed to the plan—including going back to his place.

Looking back, it may not have been the wisest thing to do for her personal safety, but this was an opportunity to leap into the dating game feet first and Tinderella was feeling footloose and fancy-free.

He arrived just after midnight and messaged her that he was parked out the front of the club. She left her bestie and jumped into his car. It was a truck really, a tradie's truck, like a Great Wall or a Toyota dual cab.

There he sat, in the driver's seat, and he looked like his pictures. Thank goodness!

Tinderella glanced at his body. He had underdressed for the occasion, in a work singlet and shorts, but his easy nature matched his outfit. It made her more relaxed, and they started to talk about general things, and she got to know a bit about him and his work. It wasn't long before they arrived at his house. It was new-looking, in a well-established area not far from the city.

Tinderella was a little nervous as they walked into the kitchen, but she didn't feel that she had made the wrong decision.

Don was very hospitable and offered her a drink. It gave her something to focus on to stop the tiny little nerves that were developing. Fresh out of a long-term relationship, she suddenly felt every bit of her lack of experience when it came to dating—and especially making herself vulnerable with an unfamiliar man.

But here she was, the plan she had masterminded unfolding.

They moved to the bedroom and Tinderella took off her silver heels, which in all honesty was much better because Don was very short. He guided her to the bed and gently began to seduce her. He was respectful in his technique and caring with his words, and she knew that she had chosen the right guy for her 'first time'.

The sex happened, it was pretty standard, and she caught an Uber back to her place. Tinderella realised that it was simply a sexual encounter—no more, no less. It wasn't crazy exciting or different to what she'd known before. She was honest enough to admit to herself later on that, at that point, she hadn't known the difference between sex and making love. With Don, she'd just had sex with a stranger so she could tick a box. He didn't seem too perturbed by this obvious intent and neither was she. They were two consenting adults doing something together that happened to be sex.

And she *had* done it! She was now an empowered woman! Not because the sex had been amazing, but because she'd actually had a one-night stand! She felt free and confident.

As it turned out, the best part of this story wasn't the sex. It was what happened after…

The following morning Tinderella called her girlfriend Eliza to tell her she'd successfully completed her first one-night stand. She spoke with great enthusiasm, recounting every detail about the night before and including all the juicy details; the long text exchanges on Tinder to arrange their meet up, the midnight pick up, his nice nature, his job and where he lived.

Eliza listened quietly and then asked, 'Is his name Don?'

You could have heard a pin drop, and the silence seemed endless as Tinderella tried to process the question and put two and two together. She listened intently as Eliza explained the story of her relationship with Don.

Eliza had met him through Tinder, too, and had been talking to him for the past two weeks. She'd thought a genuine relationship had formed between the two of them. In online terms, they had progressed to 'second base', as their conversations had moved to texting on the phone. Tinderella started to feel nauseous as Eliza explained *her* night before.

On Tinderella's big date night, Eliza had also been communicating with Don on the phone for quite a while, and he had been asking her to meet with him. She'd had very little power left on her phone battery and was nervous about driving to Don's house because she had not yet met him in person. She was worried that if her battery died on the way, she would get lost and be stranded, so she had decided against meeting up with him that night. They had continued to chat, though, until Don said he had to go, and they agreed to talk again soon.

Unbeknownst to Eliza, Don had been texting with Tinderella at the same time! He 'had to go' to pick Tinderella up and take her back to his home.

What where the chances? The two friends couldn't believe their misfortune! Tinderella felt terrible about the situation, but Eliza was very matter of fact.

'These things happen in the dating game—but hopefully not too often,' she said, and after a few awkward giggles they both felt better.

Not prepared to let Don off scott-free, however, Eliza sent him a message shortly after, saying she'd heard he had had a good night. Don had no idea—at least until Eliza explained he'd slept with one of her best friends! He started to apologise to Eliza about the whole mix up, texting that he had instantly regretted his choice.

Tinderella also received a message from Don, asking her to speak to Eliza and explain that he really did care about her and regretted the choice he had made. Oh, the drama! Tinderella couldn't believe what she was hearing.

What the heck are you talking to other women for, if you're truly interested in Eliza, she thought. She was well and truly caught in the middle of a complicated situation she had never anticipated or wanted. She did as Don asked and passed his message along to Eliza, feeling as if she was back in the schoolyard, passing notes. Don likes Eliza, Eliza likes Don, but Don stuffed up and now he wants Eliza back … Oh, she needed a wine, but it was way too early in the day to drink.

Eliza agreed to reconcile with Don. They were all consenting adults, after all, and if what they were feeling was a real connection, maybe they could meet for a drink and talk it through.

They met, and it ended on the spot.

Eliza called Tinderella afterwards to tell her that, even though Don was nice, and he was sincerely sorry, she couldn't get past how short he was. Tinderella can only guess what you're all thinking... How superficial!

But it's a woman's choice and if tall is what floats her friend's boat, it's her call!

Tinderella couldn't believe the chances of something like this happening, but the good news is her friendship with Eliza was maintained and she had achieved her one-night stand icebreaker!

Crisis averted! Phew...

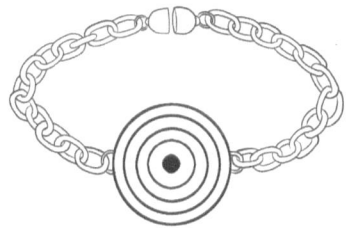

It's Time to Talk... by Simone

KNOW YOUR ONLINE DATING GOALS

To get the best from online dating, think about what you want to achieve and how. Are you looking for love, sex, friendship or all three? Do you have a timeframe in mind or are you happy to take your time and go on the odd date? Some dating sites offer discounts for paid memberships depending on the duration of your sign-up period. What about the number of people you wish to see at any time—do you want to date one guy, or a few in a row, or multiple guys at once?

Take the time to think about and even write down your expectations and planned approach to online dating—before you begin the process.

Plan your dating journey

Just like physical travel, your dating journey requires planning, and commitment. Ask yourself if you're truly ready for this. If you've been single for some time, you may find that you will need to make changes in your life to welcome in a life partner, or even an expanded social life. Much of your free time will now be spent talking with and meeting numerous men. Be prepared for the time and effort you will need to invest along the way before arriving at your destination—whether that's finding a playmate or your soul mate.

Dating really is a numbers game and if you're fortunate to meet your soul mate early in your journey, the number of people you need to date will be fewer than you had perhaps planned—or feared.

Of course, before physical dating comes the standard online messaging, texting and phone calls. These activities also require an outlay of your time. As with any investment, the more you invest, the higher the return. Just remember to invest as much time and care in yourself as you do in your dates.

Planning checklist
- Plan in advance how much of your time you want to invest in your dating journey. As a guide, set aside at least one night a week or fortnight as your 'date' night and one morning or afternoon on a weekend as your 'coffee date' meetings.
- Don't start your dating journey while you have a lot going on in your life or you're planning a major event. You don't want to be stressed or tired when talking online to someone, or find yourself unable to arrange a meeting with a potential match because of your busy schedule.
- If you have children or other dependents living with you, talk with them about your journey—to the level and depth of what you want to share with them—to avoid potential resistance and to secure their support for you on the journey you're about to embark on.
- If you have young children, decide who you want to babysit them—whether these are paid babysitters or friends/family. Set this up in advance so you have budgeted to pay a babysitter every week or weekend for the next month or two (or the timeframe you've planned). Alternatively, set up a schedule in advance with friends and family so you don't feel guilty about leaning on them to look after your kids. If you're feeling hesitant to impose, remember most people enjoy helping, especially when there is something specific for them to offer. They are more likely to be supportive of you for having the courage to put yourself out there and want to help you by minding your kids than not. You may not need babysitters as often as weekly or fortnightly, but at least you've planned for it.

Take control of your online world.

Once your profile goes live a whole new world beckons and you are likely to be overwhelmed by the number of potential suitors who contact you or who are recommended as a match for you.

You will be 'poked', 'starred', 'swiped', 'heart-ed' and more. What a fabulous boost to your ego!

This is when it pays to have a plan because you can easily spend a lot of time online responding to messages and engaging in conversations. Like all social media channels, online dating apps can be a major time-suck, particularly if you find yourself 'waiting by the phone' for someone to respond to you. That part of the dating game hasn't changed much, although people today tend to expect much faster response times than in the days of landlines and snail mail. You may choose to invest a lot of time interacting regularly with people online or jump on and off sites in bursts of days or weeks.

Along the way, it's important to keep focused on other things in your life that make you happy, so that your source of joy is not just from receiving positive comments and matches. Keep a realistic and balanced perspective about online dating.

When to take the next step—and the next

The move from online to meeting in person is an exciting one. Some people are happy to go from chatting online to meeting in person and others prefer to speak over the phone first before meeting up. Do whatever is comfortable for you. You could meet at a coffee shop, a restaurant or in a park. Where you meet is up to you, but make sure that this arrangement is something you feel truly comfortable with. The more relaxed you are, the more natural you will be with your date.

Before deciding to progress from a first date to a second date, consider if you had any niggling doubts after your first meeting. Only meet with him again if you want to determine whether your hesitations and doubts were warranted, or whether these could be put down to nerves—his or yours. Keep checking in with yourself after each date—listen to your intuition. It often knows before your conscious mind does.

If you don't feel a 'spark' or any attraction after your first date it is okay to turn him down if he asks you for a second date. Yes, he may feel rejected, but it's not up to you to manage or alleviate his emotional responses. Be polite and respectful, as you would wish to be treated.

If you feel the attraction is mutual, then it may be during the second date (or a later one, as suits you) that you discuss your relationship expectations and why you are drawn to him. A person's profile would usually provide an early indication of expectations, however expectations may change if two people really hit it off, so it's crucial to keep checking in. The conversation itself around expectations will provide you with interesting insights into the man you are dating and his suitability (or not) as a friend, lover or life partner.

When to discuss being exclusive

If it matters to you, then it's also okay to ask if your date is happy to keep seeing you on an exclusive basis. If the answer is 'yes', then you know you've got someone worth continuing to keep seeing. If the answer is 'no', then it's up to you to determine whether you're willing to keep seeing a guy who has, by his response, indicated that they're actually not sure if you're 'the one'—or they just want to keep their options open.

Be aware that some are just not looking for love with a capital L. Tinderella's experience with Don uncovered the dishonest behaviour of a 'player'. Fortunately, she caught him out early, before her heart—or the other woman's—was on the line. Not everyone online is looking for a genuine, monogamous and long-term relationship. Some people are happy to look for sex or friendship or a 'friends with benefits' arrangement. If the latter are your goals for online dating, then poly-dating is likely to be a perfect strategy for you.

MAKE A LIST—AND CHECK IT TWICE

When you decide to date, you need to be clear on what you want and don't want in a man. Just like writing down New Year's resolutions, write down your list of what you want in a guy: his character traits, how he treats you, how his friends/family treat you, his work ethics, hobbies/interests, attitude towards health/wellbeing, and more.

Your list reflects your own needs and values, and while we are all only human, and therefore flawed, your list is a tangible reminder of what you will and won't tolerate in a relationship. Be as specific as you can—it's your list!

It can be easy—and fun—to make a list at a conscious level of all the things we're looking for in a partner. Honesty is high on every woman's list. On an unconscious level, we tend to look for people who have character traits we don't see in ourselves. This is probably a good thing, otherwise we'd all be in relationships with people who are the same as us and life would be pretty boring. Having said this, differing traits are often a cause for challenge and conflict in relationships because they govern how we act, and how we communicate and interact with others. Understanding our own and others' character traits can help us to more easily mesh with others and maintain our relationships.

Values are as important as character traits when you consider your future partner. Values drive where we put our attention and effort, and can include family, career, money, health, travel, friends and community. It is human nature to be drawn to people who share the same values as you. Common values mean you're likely to be in sync when it comes to how you spend your time together. For example, if you both value family highly, then as the relationship develops you'll be more likely to happily book in for a picnic at the zoo with the kids rather than a night at the casino.

When your values aren't in sync, and others criticise or challenge the things high on your values hierarchy, you're much more likely to be hurt or to go on the defensive. For example, if you value your friendships and your date criticises your BFF or the time you spend with her, then you will likely want to bite back.

If you're not sure what to include on your future partner 'wish list', then dating different men will help you explore what really matters to you in a potential life partner. Tinderella is constantly adding to and refining her list during her online dating journey.

Our website offers a number of free downloadable resources, including a template to help get you started on your wish list. Visit www.talesoftinderella.com and download Tinderella's *K.I.S.S. List for Mr Right* from the Resources page (K.I.S.S. stands for 'keep it simple stupid' to reflect the simplicity of this important list). Use this template to capture the character traits, values, lifestyle choices, attributes and more that you want in your potential life partner. You can add to this list over time and revisit it after every new date to help you become clearer on what you're looking for.

Write this list when you're in a positive mood and excited about your future. You'll probably learn as much about yourself as the man you are looking for, and you may find that it highlights any patterns you have had in past relationships. It's also a great exercise to do with a girlfriend or two—often your BFF knows you better than you know yourself.

The list you create will not only guide you in your choice of the men you opt to meet, it will remind you of what's important to you during moments of loneliness or uncertainty. For example, when you've been on a date with a guy who is only 'kinda' what you're looking for. Sometimes loneliness, hurt or rejection can impair our judgement. At times like these it can seem reasonable to choose to be with a guy who wants you more than you want him. This list will remind you to hang in there to meet the guy who is right for you—because he is definitely out there! Never settle for less than you deserve. Above all else, your list should include all the basics of decent human relationships such as honesty, respect, kindness

DATER BEWARE

Everyone puts their best version of themselves forward when they are dating. It is not until about three months they reveal their true selves. It's not a 'bad thing' and people are usually not consciously aware of it. This is just normal human behaviour which happens in many situations, such as starting a new job.

Two people who were recently strangers will develop an increasing sense of comfort and trust as they spend more time together. It is during this period of exploration you will be drawn closer to the guy or you will experience warning bells from your intuition, letting you know that something isn't right.

With this in mind, it's okay—and actually a good idea—to have many dates with more than one person at a time. Dating a variety of men will allow you to consider how you feel about differing personalities, life interests, passions, goals and sexual compatibility.

Some traits will seem important to you and 'feel right', while other traits may not be as important as you once thought. This serves to help you refine and build your *K.I.S.S. List for Mr Right* during your journey.

A word on personal safety

Sadly, there are people who are simply dishonest. Despite your best intentions in communicating your wishes, expectations and goals, some guys will nod and agree with you yet do the opposite if they think they can get away with it to satisfy their own needs.

While you probably won't be able to avoid this type of behaviour entirely, understanding it can happen will help you better manage your own expectations and boundaries.

Take sensible precautions when you move to physical meetings. Eliza decided not to meet with Don because she was worried her phone would die before she made it to his house. Mobile phones can provide a valuable safety net, so it's a good idea to carry a portable battery charger in your handbag. If your phone goes flat while you are on a date, you can recharge it and call a friend if you need to, check on your children, and navigate your way home. Another safety tip is to text the address of your date's home and a screen shot of his profile photo to a trusted friend before you go to his house.

LEARNINGS FROM TINDERELLA AND DON:

1. Be clear on what you want from your online dating journey. Are you looking for love, sex, friendship—or all three? Is your approach to meeting guys going to be casual and relaxed or focused and scheduled? Do you want to date one guy at a time (mono-dating) or more than one (poly-dating)? Be open and honest about this during your journey as the men you meet are people on a journey, too.

2. Determine the important qualities and attributes you want in your life partner. Use Tinderella's *K.I.S.S. List for Mr Right* (downloadable from www.talesoftinderella.com) to help get you started. Treat your dating experiences as a journey of discovery in finding a man who 'ticks all your boxes'.

3. Communicate with your dates in a way that feels comfortable to you. This includes how and where you meet your dates and how you reject offers for additional dates if the guy isn't right for you. If you've found a guy you'd like to date on an exclusive basis, then share your wishes with him—but be prepared for his response if he has a different view on this.

Chapter 3

Aaron

Problems of human behavior still continue to baffle us, but at least in the Library we have them properly filed.

- Anita Brookner

Tinderella never imagined she would meet the incestuous fantasy lover obsessed with all things 'odd'. She had a very balanced approach to sex and would never judge anyone for their sexual preferences. But then came Aaron.

This dashing man in his late forties had just been relocated to the city for a new job as work had dried up in his hometown. He had been recruited to work on the new light rail system being developed in the city. Perfect! Fresh talent interested in getting acquainted with new people in a new town. Tinderella was actually quite flattered Aaron had swiped right to be matched with her. They messaged back and forth for a few days and got on really well.

They arranged to meet at his place and walk to a local bar from there.

Tinderella caught an Uber to his apartment and took a bottle of Chandon with her to add a bit of fun to the evening. Aaron had the physique of a retired rugby player, a fuller man who was very confident in his body. He gently kissed her on the cheek as she entered the apartment.

They found themselves looking out from the balcony; the conversation flowing easily between them. Tinderella noticed there always seemed to be some kind of sexual innuendo to everything he spoke about. Aaron especially liked the little V-neck dress she was wearing. Tailored and a dark emerald-green, it was sexy and sophisticated at the same time. The dress captured her curves in every way, and she could feel his eyes on every part of her. From her butt to her breasts, Aaron's eyes were taking her all in.

She noticed his gaze lingering on her chest. Maybe it's because he's looking at my necklace, she thought. Using black ribbon, she had transformed her favourite waterhole bracelet into a necklace. The length had adjusted perfectly, and it sat just above her cleavage.

At the bar they sat close together, Aaron's leg touching Tinderella's knee. He smiled at her and she focused on her wine glass while she played with her hair, which was set in beautiful soft beachy waves that framed her face perfectly. A definite sexual chemistry was brewing.

Aaron's gaze settled on her hands, still playing with her hair. He commented on how beautiful they were, how her fingers were so long and gorgeous.

Well, this was a first for Tinderella. A lifetime of hairdressing and this was the first time anyone had commented so specifically on her hands. Tinderella was flattered.

Little did she know, he was studying the potential length of her cervix!

Apparently, from the tip of your middle finger to the first crease in your wrist is the length of your vaginal canal. Oh my God! She had thought he was being polite, talking about her nice piano fingers. Who would have expected this topic to come up in the first few minutes of meeting a date? She found it quite humorous and since Aaron was so light-hearted about it; she didn't take offence.

He continued to charm her as they had a few more drinks, his eyes sparkling with mischief. Tinderella was sold. She was keen to progress things with Aaron and see where they would end up, but there was a slight issue. She had her period. She'd never had sex whilst on her period and was absolutely not considering it on this occasion. The embarrassment of red-stained sheets? Tinderella was going to opt out of that one, thank you!

The evening continued to go well—they bar-hopped and enjoyed the different atmosphere of each venue they visited. Aaron told her all about his ex-wife, and his grown daughter who was living overseas.

Conversation was easy. Aaron made her giggle with his sense of humour and Tinderella felt comfortable in his company. He proved to be very polite around others, including the wait staff, and insisted on buying the drinks as they chatted through the night. A true gentleman.

As the evening continued there were little sneaky comments from Aaron about them ending up in bed together. The idea wasn't too far from her mind—she found him sexually arousing and he was a welcome distraction during her post-separation phase…

But no, she couldn't. She had her period and to be honest; she was silently pleased as this would prevent any activity that led to the bedroom.

Aaron suggested they head back to his apartment to finish the bottle of Chandon.

Tinderella couldn't see anything wrong with that, so she agreed.

It wasn't long before he made his move and kissed Tinderella with an open mouth and full tongue. It was a little too much for her liking, but it wasn't unbearable—yet.

Aaron guided Tinderella into the bedroom with the promise of a foot massage. How could she resist?

He placed her gently onto the bed. He peeled her lovely dress off her body with smooth expertise and he stood at the end of the bed, watching her as she lay there in her underwear.

'I can see your mouse,' he said.

She knew he was talking about her tampon string and she started to feel slightly embarrassed. Who says that? He was so bold and confident.

'Well, yes. You just leave it alone.'

Unperturbed, Aaron leant over her and gazed directly into her eyes. Tinderella could feel her knickers coming off. Oh my. She was vulnerable and totally exposed.

What was he doing?

He leant to kiss her whilst his fingers found her tampon string. She felt a slight tug on it, and he continued to pull the tampon out until it was no longer inside her.

She was in shock. This had never happened to her before!

Surely men were against sex during that time of the month?

He held her tampon up like a dead mouse and said, 'There's nothing on it, and now I'm going to fuck you!'

Tinderella was relieved that at least the tampon was clean. He went to the bathroom to bin it. She was freaking out, but curiosity—or shock—held her glued to the bed.

What was she thinking? Get up and go! But she couldn't seem to move. She stayed frozen, processing what had just happened.

Aaron returned from the bathroom and leant over her.

'I hope you're ready for my nine inches.'

Tinderella was feeling so nervous but she couldn't admit that to him. Breathe, Tinderella, breathe....

Aaron began to penetrate her and became excited very quickly. And then things got weird.

The role-play began.

'Oh, Mummy, I want to fuck you....'

Tinderella was in shock. Was this grown man pretending she was his *mother*? Holy crap!

Aaron continued to pump into her full and hard, with increasing intensity... and more references to Mummy. He wanted Mummy to take his virginity. He was hot and hard for her!

Okay, Tinderella thought, this is beyond weird.

But it wasn't over. Aaron had reached his pre-orgasm state and then he came with such powerful thrusts, he was obviously in a state of ecstasy. His voice took on a higher pitch, and he was yelling, 'Mummy! Mummy!'

Tinderella could hardly believe what she'd witnessed. This guy had just gotten off imagining she was his Mummy! Tinderella wasn't overly experienced, but she knew this was *not* her thing.

So, she gathered her clothes, left the apartment and went home.

The next day, Aaron began to call and message her every hour.

He told her of his fantasies and what he wanted to do to her, and the character he wanted her to be in bed—his perfect role-play. When Aaron said he wanted her to be his thirteen-year-old daughter, so he could visit her bedroom and take her virginity whilst she was experiencing her first menstrual bleed, Tinderella was through with him.

She was in shock.

Enough was enough. It had to end.

And it did. Good riddance.

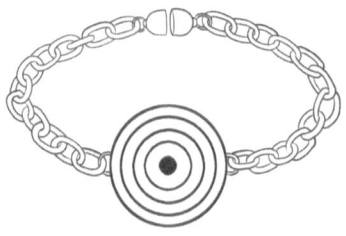

***It's Time to Talk…* by Simone**

HUMAN SEXUALITY AND FANTASY

You will meet all sorts when you're dating. Like many other lifestyle choices, sexual fantasies are a matter of personal taste. They may be your thing, they may not, but either way if a guy you're having sex with launches directly into a fantasy without first discussing his intentions, you may understandably feel very uncomfortable. This is what we witnessed between Aaron and Tinderella. He may have been nervous about how Tinderella would respond, or he cared only for his own sexual gratification—we'll examine boundaries in a moment.

Generally speaking, sexual fantasies are totally normal and a great way to explore your sexuality in a space that's super safe—your imagination. Our thoughts can induce physical changes in our bodies. For example, when you think of a delicious meal, your mouth waters and your tummy rumbles. When you feel anger, your body tenses up. In the bedroom, thinking about things, people or situations that arouse you makes your body respond in a pleasurable way, intensifying your sexual experience and orgasms. If you love role-playing or are curious to experience it, then go for it! It's a fabulous way to spice up your sex life and to explore what turns you on with a willing sexual partner.

Establish healthy boundaries in the bedroom

Exploring your sexuality can be an exciting and joyful part of your dating journey. If sexual fantasies and fetishes are something you're interested in, it is essential you feel safe at all times and establish some clear boundaries—whether you're having sex with a guy you've just met, or he is someone you know well.

It's important to agree beforehand what you are both going to do as part of the fantasy or 'scene' you're creating, what you might be willing to do and what you absolutely will not do. This list defines your boundaries. Respect these boundaries and insist your partner does too. Don't be afraid to discuss any instances where he may want to test or stretch your boundaries. Negotiate what feels right for you. You can always revisit this as you further explore your sexuality. When it comes to sex, it's your choice what you want to do or not do. Your boundaries will keep you firmly in control in the bedroom to ensure you enjoy your sexual experiences.

If he asks you to explore a fantasy or fetish you are uncomfortable with, then raise your concerns with him and have a discussion to determine what you can accommodate—and what you won't. If your partner launches into a role playing sexual fantasy or a fetish you feel uncomfortable with, it's **definitely OK to not be OK** with that. Know you can voice your concerns and if needed, stop the sex immediately if you don't want to continue.

Even if you really like the guy, it is okay to reject the behaviour. You are not rejecting the person. How he responds to this discussion indicates how much he respects you.

If he tries to convince you or coerce you to do the role playing, then he is not respecting your boundaries—or you! This could be a deal breaker, so you'll need to be ready with your 'smooth exit' words. Unlike leaving a guy at a bar or public place, you'll need some words better suited for extracting yourself from the bedroom.

First and foremost is your personal safety. If you don't feel safe, tell him that the night is over, collect your belongings and leave (or tell him to leave if he's at your home). If you just want out, perhaps tell him you're no longer 'in the mood' and want to call it a night. If he's not okay with your objections or concerns, then perhaps it's time to consider whether to continue seeing this person.

GOOD FANTASY, BAD FANTASY

Interestingly (or shockingly, depending on your perceptions), mother-focused sex fantasies are more common than you might expect. It is probably the most taboo act a man could carry out, which in itself can be powerfully erotic for a guy. But it's certainly not a commonly accepted fantasy, because if it was, more men would be talking about it. If you are interested to know more, Sigmund Freud's theory of the Oedipus Complex will explain its origin in more detail.

Aaron's fantasy about having sex with his 13-year-old virginal daughter, however, would be considered paedophilic, given the specific details of an incestuous relationship and the child being under the age of consent.

There are various causes of paedophilia, including abnormalities in hormones; serotonin brain chemicals; and genetics or learned behaviour (particularly when there are generational instances of paedophilia).

Aaron's fantasies about having sex with his mother and sex with a child/his own daughter are possible indicators he may, as a child himself, have been the victim or the observer of inappropriate sexual behaviours or otherwise experienced generalised trauma. Research has shown that when a child experiences extreme levels of abuse, this can result in having inappropriate sexual boundaries and desires as an adult[5]. Aaron may have experienced such trauma as a child as he had no issue with taking Tinderella on his Oedipal and paedophilic fantasy ride even though he had never met her before. He simply assumed Tinderella would want to explore similar fantasies with him, which indicated he did not have appropriate boundaries or a sense of sexual normalcy.

Aaron is likely to struggle to meet a woman who would be comfortable with his darker fantasies, yet it's also possible he could let go of these through the support of a qualified therapist or psychologist.

SOME ADVICE ON SAFE SEX

No matter what sexual positions or role playing you enjoy, the most important consideration is to adopt and enforce safe sex. People often falsely assume they are 'clean' or free of disease because they've been with the same partner for many years before their rela-

---

[5] https://www.ncbi.nlm.nih.gov/pubmed/2082860

tionship ended. In fact, statistics are showing that the rate of sexually transmitted infections (STIs) being contracted by people in the 45+ age group is increasing each year[6].

It's quite common for people to have a LOT of sex after they leave long-term relationships, so be safe sex aware! Serious STIs are easily spread through having sex, including chlamydia, gonorrhoea, syphilis, human immunodeficiency virus (HIV), genital herpes, hepatitis B, human papillomavirus (HPV) and trichomonas. Some of these diseases can have devastating lifelong health implications. The only way to avoid a sexually transmitted infection is by insisting your partner wears a condom. Techniques to prevent pregnancy such as withdrawing before ejaculation or using a spermicide do not offer protection against STIs.

It is highly likely you'll meet guys who say they don't like wearing condoms, or that they don't have any available. Be prepared and carry your own condoms whenever you go on a date. If you haven't used them before, take one out of its packet and practice applying it on to a zucchini (yes—just like the sex educators do in high school!). Also, be ready with a few words to prompt your guy when it comes time to use a condom. You can keep it simple and direct, 'Would you like me to help you put on a condom?'

Keep practicing safe sex until such time you and your guy are exclusive. Before you stop using condoms, you should both consider having STI checks through your doctor or sexual health clinic.

LEARNINGS FROM TINDERELLA AND AARON

1. Sexual fantasies can be a great way to spice up your sex life. Don't be afraid to explore what turns you on.

---

[6] https://www.cdc.gov/std/stats16/default.htm

2. Discuss fantasies with your guy and only participate if you feel comfortable. Some fantasies can be quite dark so it's okay to say no to them, or to the guy generally.
3. Remember—safe sex, always!

Chapter 4

Jackson

You can't run from your past. You'll end up running in circles. Until you fall back down into the same hole you were trying to escape from, only the hole's grown deeper.

— Max Payne

There's always that one guy who teaches you about love. Jackson was that guy for Tinderella. This date swipe turned into one of her most heart breaking relationships. She fell in love—hook, line, sinker and boat. This chapter brought a few tears to her eyes as she wrote it, and it wrung her heart out like an old towel. But it's a story Tinderella needs to tell.

It all started when she came across a handsome, confident man with the most unbelievable smile. You know, the guy who makes your heart skip a beat, and you check your dating app profile every ten minutes hoping he will swipe right and match with you.

Jackson was tall at 6'4", with a three-day growth and a closely shaven scalp. He was a landscaper, a real tradesman—always a win in Tinderella's book.

Oh, Tinderella knows what you are thinking!

Trust her, she thought the same thing.

But she hasn't finished yet; Jackson also had the best guns, a nice chest, and tattoos.

I hear you. What more could any girl want?

Jackson was also a great cook, and a single dad who shared custody of his son every second week.

Tinderella wanted to meet this guy. She swiped right, and it wasn't long before she received a notification. They'd matched!

She nearly peed her pants... they started messaging each other, finding out a bit more about each other every time they connected. He was smart and funny. Tinderella hadn't met him in person but it was great to see his intelligence come through in his messages. And the best part? He was grammatically correct! Oh, this guy was a dream.

They chatted about his job as a landscaper and how he loved being on the tools. He spoke of his love for his son and how he had been a bit of a rebel and a troublemaker in his younger years. He was the bad boy we all love to love.

Jackson was a likeable fellow, always smiling, and he made a point of sending Tinderella a lovely good morning message every day. He was the type of guy who would give you the shirt off his back, warm you with his jacket and hold the car door open for you. From the beginning, it was clear to see his love language was 'acts of service'.

After about a week of chatting through the day and into the night, Tinderella decided to call and ask him for a drink.

He was very clever in his response, saying, 'So now it's the interview, is it?'

It made Tinderella giggle, and they locked in a date. At this point, they had only been communicating through messages. She definitely wanted to get to know this guy ASAP. They chose to meet in a local bar not too far from either of them, making it easy to meet in the middle.

During the drive, she glanced at the waterhole bracelet gleaming on her wrist. It seemed to be a part of her now, and she wore it on every date. She hoped it was a lucky omen. She was only casually dressed, as she had not had time to go home and get changed for the date. She reassured herself that her comfy blue jeans and her new cotton off-the-shoulder lace top still looked good with her high cream boots; even though she'd be a little windblown by the time she got there. As an extra precaution against the changeable weather, she had also brought her brown leather jacket.

Tinderella pulled her car into the bar carpark and looked at her watch. She'd texted Jackson to let him know she'd be late, but she'd run over by more than an hour. She walked inside and took a seat at a hightop table set with bar stools and waited. She looked at her phone. No message from Jackson, so she sent him a text asking where he was. He said he was outside. Butterflies played in her stomach as she walked to meet him. She saw him standing there and her heart literally skipped a beat. He was wearing a smart jacket over snug-fitting jeans and he was physically appealing to her in every way. Oh, I am in trouble with this one, she thought.

They decided to go inside to have a drink and chat. They connected straight away on a nice, easy level. She could hardly have explained the mixed emotions that were charging through her. This guy stimulated her body and her mind and set alight every sexual fantasy Tinderella had ever dreamed of.

Before she knew it, three hours had passed, and they had not run out of conversation. They had covered every topic known to man and still could have kept going. Finally, they had to say their goodbyes, and he gave her a very soft, polite kiss on the lips. Oh, Tinderella so wanted more! They agreed to see each other again, and she was secretly over the moon.

In the six months during which they saw each other, they had three break ups.

The first came not long after Tinderella announced their relationship online, for the whole world to see—and the trolling started.

She received private messages from several women who Jackson dated previously with accusations that unsettled her and made her question her judgement of his character. A new woman began to post further accusations online. Tinderella was devastated and shocked to say the least. Who was this guy? She and Jackson didn't have any mutual friends, so it was difficult for her to confirm or discredit these accusations. It didn't stop there.

The anonymous woman found Tinderella's contact number and rang her.

Tinderella was on the phone to this woman for the next few minutes, asking her to provide some actual examples of the accusations she was making. There were a lot of attacks on his character, but not much else. Oh, this was getting messy! What was Tinderella to think? She didn't know what to do or say. Her emotions were already involved—she was stuck on him.

She was worried about what to do. Should she trust him, or take the word of others who obviously had an agenda and a deep resentment for him? Tinderella asked the advice of her closest girlfriends—and they were worried, too. After much thought, she decided to tell Jackson she needed to have a break as this was getting too close to home. This anonymous troll was obviously stalking her to have been able to find her personal number.

Tinderella needed to take a step back.

Jackson agreed to the break, but while her head was saying 'let it go', her heart was saying something else... She spoke to his parents, and they agreed it was a bitter personal attack. Tinderella needed to ignore the false accusations. So, with caution, they began to see each other again, even as doubts still niggled within her. She ignored her usually correct intuition.

As the relationship continued, the ups and downs meant she could never quite banish that doubt. Jackson could be fabulous and enthusiastic, yet at other times he seemed dark and distant. As time went on, his insecurities and moods became more and more common, and their differences began to surface.

Tinderella was able to talk to a close guy friend who could give her a male perspective on her problems. Tinderella couldn't understand why Jackson felt so frustrated and threatened by this. She was very social and enjoyed going out, whether it was going to a club, dinner or just drinks; he preferred to stay home and hibernate, and often made comments about how much he disliked people and socializing.

Tinderella decided she needed a new look and with her hairdresser friend's support, planned to make a bold colour change from brunette to bronze, which she had never done before. She shared this with Jackson on the phone.

'I'm going to look as hot as Jennifer Lopez,' she teased.

His reply was, 'Babe, you're hot, but you'll never be as hot as her.'

She needed a moment to digest his statement. He didn't retract it and her reaction was swift. She hung up on him. Later that week, as they were lying together in his bed chatting, Jackson told Tinderella she had flaws. They weren't arguing; it was just a blunt statement.

Fair enough. Who doesn't? Everyone has flaws!

Tinderella knew she had her fair share, but to hear it from someone who was meant to be her protector, her boyfriend? It hurt. She rolled over, her body language making it clear she objected to his comment and it had hurt her. It was such an unfair attack. Hot tears ran down her face and she cried silently. Wasn't this meant to be the guy who was to protect her and love her unconditionally? Her future soul mate?

It's funny how the universe works. At that moment her phone vibrated with a message from her son, which gave her a reason to go home and leave the situation behind. Jackson wasn't happy about it and reacted rudely. In hindsight, she realised he didn't like to share her and wanted her fully to himself. This was not something she could give him. She was an independent woman, very committed to her two children, and had to share her world between the ones she loved and the man she was getting to know.

As you can probably tell, the cracks in this relationship were starting to show. Between the actions of the online trolls and the pressure to change her lifestyle, along with the little personal digs,

Tinderella began to question whether the good times of this relationship made it worthwhile. Reflecting on their time together, she realised she had become an emotional, financial and parental ATM to Jackson, and she couldn't do it anymore.

But she had a challenge. The upsides of the relationship were incredible. Jackson was great company when he wanted to be. He was dynamic and talented in so many ways—including in bed. The sex was mind blowing! He had brought her to orgasm more times than she'd had late nights. The downside was that he was possessive, and his mind games were messing with her head. Was great sex a good enough reason to stay with someone? It was tempting, but her mind was her real stimulant, and it was getting screwed in a different way.

Get a grip, Tinderella, and sort yourself out!

Arghhh! I'm trying, she thought.

She had a few mantras she lived by and one of them seemed really relevant at this time, 'If this were happening to a girlfriend, what advice would Tinderella give her?' She knew the answer. She would tell her to keep looking rather than settle for mediocre.

The next day, Jackson called her, trying to talk it through, but she wouldn't have a bar of it. Experience had taught Tinderella a few things, and she knew she had to stand her ground.

This was not an easy conversation. Over the weekend, they spoke on the phone, they cried, they declared their love for each other, and then came the blame game; who did this, and who did that. The block between them was ridiculous. Even when they started to see each other again, they seemed to never be on the same page. If Tinderella was upset, Jackson would get upset, rather than talk the problem through and try to meet in the middle. He would take everything so personally, and in the end Tinderella found herself walking on eggshells, having to be careful with everything she said.

She finally knew it was over when she noticed a band she loved was coming to town and she desperately wanted to go—but she didn't want to take Jackson with her. Alarm bells started ringing. She had taken him to a previous concert, and he had hated it. They didn't seem to share the same taste in music, and when Jackson wasn't interested, he made it very difficult for those around him to have a good time. His eyes would glaze over and cast a shadow of darkness Tinderella had never seen in anyone before.

They parted ways, but then the worst happened. Jackson lost a family member, someone very dear to him. This loss broke his heart and took him to the pits of darkness.

Tinderella was devastated for him. He told her he had no one else to call, and that was sad within itself, as he had alienated himself from many friends over the years. She wanted to be there for him as a friend, so she would call him. He wouldn't answer. She would message him, and he would reply with emotional distance. She would get upset and react when he ignored her calls. She would plead to talk with him… no answer… and the vicious cycle went on.

Tinderella needed clarity and perspective on how to move forward in her life. She saw a psychic. The minute she sat down, the psychic told her she intimidated Jackson and explained everything about why the two of them couldn't, and wouldn't, work. Tinderella was speechless. She was in awe of this reading and relieved at the outcome. The psychic's words strengthened her resolve and allowed her to believe this door needed to be closed. She needed to be strong and stay away. This decision had to be about what would be best for her, rather than how she could help Jackson.

It was the bittersweet confirmation she needed that it was over.

The following day she received a message from Jackson. He had promised to call the night before, and she had waited… but, nothing.

He finally asked, 'Are you OK?'

Tinderella replied, 'Jackson, no—I am not okay. But I will be. I have to leave this relationship/friendship or whatever it has become. I'm tired of it. Goodbye, Jackson—I am finally finished.'

It was done.

Tinderella had to be strong, for herself—and for him. She was done for the good of both of them. Moving forward, would she open her heart again? She hoped she would be lucky enough to get that chance.

Besides, there was always Tinder.

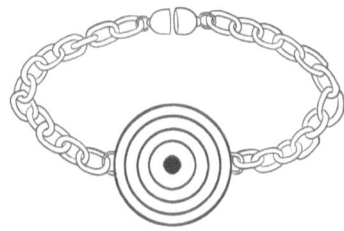

It's Time to Talk... by Simone

DEFINE A HEALTHY RELATIONSHIP

It's safe to say that most of us embark on our online dating journey looking for love. But if you haven't experienced a loving, healthy relationship before now, it can be tricky to know what one looks and feels like, beyond those portrayed in Hollywood movies.

In Chapter 2, we talked about creating a wish list of the qualities and traits you are looking for in a man - your *K.I.S.S. List for Mr Right* (see my section "Make a List and Check it Twice"). However, it's just as important to know what you are looking for in a relationship: how you want to feel when you're together; how you want to be treated by him; how you will both handle conflict and disagreements; what you will enjoy doing together as a couple; what goals you want to share as a couple; what your shared views are on family, children, finances, travel, and more.

Below is a list of the qualities and traits of a healthy relationship. It's by no means definitive, but may provide some prompts for your own list.

Healthy relationships checklist

- You support each other through all of life's ups and downs and you help each other work through personal challenges without judgement.
- You keep your own identity within the relationship and so does your partner.
- You and your partner feel safe communicating personal needs and wants.
- You respect each other's differences even if you disagree on important issues. If necessary, you agree to disagree, or you find ways to compromise.

- You share realistic expectations of the relationship, not what you wish or fantasise it to be.
- You and your partner are on the same page in terms of your values and life goals.
- There is a strong sense of trust, openness and honesty between you.
- You genuinely enjoy each other's company, at least most of the time.

KNOW YOUR LOVE LANGUAGE

Just as there are many languages in countries around the world to help people communicate their wants and needs, there are 'love languages' that help people communicate their wants and needs within relationships. Gary Chapman's books on this topic are well worth reading[7]. His first book, *The Five Love Languages: How to Express Heartfelt Commitment to Your Mate*, explains we all have a preferred way of expressing love, and a preferred way of how we want others to express their love to us. His five 'love languages' are Words of Affirmation; Acts of Service; Receiving Gifts; Quality Time; and Physical touch. Tinderella guessed that Jackson's love language was 'acts of service'.

What do you think is your preferred love language? It's worth knowing this so you can share this with your potential partner. He may be speaking a different 'language' to you and has been showing his love and appreciation to you in his preferred language—not yours.

WHEN TO END A RELATIONSHIP—FOR GOOD

It's not always a bad thing to break up and get back together. In fact, for some couples, breaking up can help each realise the value of

---

[7] https://www.5lovelanguages.com/

their relationship and result in a strengthened connection and commitment between them.

However, staying in a relationship that's not working, despite the best efforts of one or both parties to fix what's broken, can be soul-destroying. One or both parties may be holding onto the fantasy of a loving relationship rather than the broken reality.

There are many reasons people stay in broken relationships, as seen in 'separated under the one roof' arrangements. This is particularly evident when there are children or business/financial complications.

The negative cycle of repeatedly breaking up and reuniting can affect a person's confidence, self-esteem, outlook on life and ultimately, their mental health. If you've broken up with someone and are considering going back to them, think carefully before making that decision. Ask yourself:

1. What are the reasons we broke up?
2. What is the likelihood those reasons will still be a problem, or could become a problem again, if we get back together?
3. Is this a toxic relationship disguised by lust?
4. Is this relationship negatively affecting my mental or physical wellbeing?
5. Am I minimising my own needs by going back or putting his needs higher than my own?
6. Am I making too many compromises by going back?

Trust your intuition. If you were giving advice to a close friend, a sister or a daughter in the same situation, what would you tell her? Be as protective of yourself as you would be of others you care for.

DEALING WITH THE CRAZY EX

You may come across men who tell you they have a 'crazy ex'. When a guy you're dating starts talking about his ex in this way, keep in mind that there are always two sides to every story.

Unless a person's previous partner has a diagnosed mental illness, their actions are more likely to indicate emotional pain than mental illness. Overwhelming pain or anger are normal feelings post-break up, and it may take a while for an ex to process these and regain their equilibrium.

When an ex isn't able to process and let go of painful feelings, their actions can escalate. At that point, some people are indeed plagued by the unwanted affections or attention of a past partner or failed date. They may receive drunken calls or texts from this person in the evenings, or they may find themselves being stalked on Facebook and social media. As in Jackson's case, some may try to thwart their ex from experiencing happiness in a new relationship and even go as far as to contact the new partner to scare them off. These types of behaviours border on mental illness and are a cause for concern regarding your own personal safety.

In Jackson's case, where an ex has gone to such lengths to dissuade someone new from seeing him, then this situation also raises the question of why he hasn't addressed this before now. Tinderella would be within her rights to ask what happened in his relationship with his ex that resulted in her feeling so compelled to warn future girlfriends against him?

Try to keep an open mind, and be mindful it is easy to accept your new guy's version of events or to take his side when he is talking about his experiences with his ex-partner. Without speaking directly with her, and perhaps even if you do, you will never know the true, unbiased version of events. Caution is key. Watch for any red flags that could indicate your date is not taking responsibility for his role in the breakdown of previous relationships. This is a trait you want to avoid in a partner when it comes to future disagreements you may have with him.

Toxic ex action checklist

If an ex is truly proving to be an intrusive and highly volatile thorn in your new partner's side or yours, you can take steps to ensure that person stays out of both your lives. The person who was actually in the relationship with the troublesome ex should:

- Cease all contact with the ex. The only exception is if there are shared parenting arrangements. In that situation, and wherever possible, only communicate in writing (emails/texts). Avoid emotional language.
- If you share children, seek mediation through family mediation or family dispute resolution to establish boundaries around communication and contact.
- If your attempts at mediation are unsuccessful, seek the legal options available to you. In the Australian Capital Territory, for example, you can apply for a Protection Order through the Magistrates Court. This document contains conditions which prevent the ex from contacting, approaching or harassing you or your partner. Depending on where you live it may be called an intervention, restraining or apprehended violence order.
- If the above actions do not achieve the desired outcome, you may need to contact the police.

DEALING WITH TOXIC MIND GAMES

Tinderella recognised the pattern of the mind games being played by Jackson and noticed how this impacted her physical and mental wellbeing. Being on the receiving end of mind games can be extremely detrimental to a person's confidence, self-esteem and sanity. It's possible people who play mind games may not know they are doing this, but they can also be calculated and manipulative in their actions.

Mind games checklist

- Unreliable contact: not texting or calling when he says he will or ignoring you when you try to contact him. When this happens repeatedly, he is essentially sending you a message that your time is not as valuable as his, or worse, that he gets a kick out of making you wait until he makes contact.
- Making you jealous: openly admiring a woman in front of you in a way that makes you feel jealous or insecure. When a guy does this, he is likely to be insecure himself and wants to feel desirable to multiple women, or he gets an ego kick out of making you feel you are 'lucky' to be with him.
- Silent treatment: ignoring you or withholding affection from you. This may be because he has low self-esteem and needs validation of his desirability, or he needs constant reassurance of your affections towards him. When you keep trying to reach out to him it makes him feel good about himself.
- Love bombing: bombarding you with words and actions of love. This can be flattering, but it can also be intended to win you over so you 'dive right in' to a committed relationship. After a period of time, his actions may ease off and you are left to wonder if he still feels the same way, or if you made the right choice in being with him in the first place. Sometimes he will love bomb you then lose interest and move on to the next woman because what he loves is the thrill of the chase.
- Ticking bomb: overly reacting or being super-sensitive to things you say. This can leave you feeling you have to watch everything you say or do so you don't upset him or trigger his temper. This is emotionally controlling behav-

iour, resulting in you feeling as if you are 'walking on eggshells' around him.

- Gaslighting: saying or doing things to make you question your sanity. He will lie and deny things and even accuse you of things to the extent you begin to question your memory or actions. This is usually done because he is trying to cover his tracks about deceitful behaviours or actions he doesn't want you to find out about. Forms of gaslighting include:
    - Lying to you (even when you have proof)
    - Telling you things (usually deceitful or deliberate distortion of the facts) that make you doubt the loyalty of your friends or family
    - Telling you that you're too emotional, sensitive or neurotic and implying what you're seeing as a problem isn't one, you just have faulty judgement
    - Accusing you of being the one who is cheating or lying
    - Belittling the things you love and making you feel these are not as valuable or important as you believe—whether these are your friendships, your career, your hobbies, etc.

If you find yourself starting to doubt your intuition or your judgement and are second guessing yourself, then it's possible you're being gaslighted. This is one of the more serious mind games one person can play against another. It's highly likely the person gaslighting you will continue to deny any accusations you may have about their behaviour or actions, or even polite requests for clarification on things that just don't add up. Unfortunately, the only way to regain your sanity is to walk away. Cut contact so you can begin healing and rebuilding your confidence.

If you suspect you are with a guy who is playing mind-games, call him on it. He may be genuinely shocked at his own behaviour and the impact it is having you on. Or, he may deny he's playing mind games, which is a mind-game in itself (gaslighting). If this is the case, it may be time to fold and call it a day on this relationship.

LEARNINGS FROM TINDERELLA AND JACKSON:

1. If there are reasons why a relationship didn't work, carefully consider those reasons before going back to him. It's easy to remember the good times and the reasons that drew you together in the first place, but unless you recognise the cause of the breakup, going back to a broken relationship can be fraught with problems. Not only could the same problems re-surface, but an on again/off again relationship can negatively impact your mental health.

2. Beware the crazy ex. Consider just their actions but look deeper to understand why the ex is still a problem for the guy you are dating. The ex may have a legitimate mental health illness, but if she tries to warn you off her ex, she may genuinely be looking out for her fellow sister to save you from sadness and pain. Trust your intuition and if you feel there's more to the story, then carefully explore this with your guy.

3. You're looking for love on this journey—not mind-games. Recognise the behaviours that are mind games and if you suspect this is happening, call him on it. If he's a player, he'll just use another mind game to explain away such behaviours. You know what to do.

Chapter 5

Ben

'All that effort,' he mused, 'merely to avoid me. How gratifying.'
- Shana Abé, The Smoke Thief

This is one of Tinderella's Fuck Me experiences.

Attempting to date 'the slippery one' was one of Tinderella's most frustrating experiences.

Ben was that guy who sends proclamations of love and keen interest, but somehow, you never get to meet him. The communication falters, he hides out for a bit and you start to write him off and then, bingo! He pops up on your message feed again.

He was a master at leading a woman on and leaving her hanging, time and time again. Tinderella, with her soft heart and gentle empathy, she seemed to be a sucker for punishment by this type, over and over again.

Ben was very good looking, tall with dark sexy features, like a cross between George Clooney and Jake Gyllenhaal. Are you getting the picture? And yes, you can drool if you need to.

Tinderella met him online about a year into her dating journey. He was charming and witty and quickly caught her attention. As they chatted away, she realised they had a mutual friend. Later she would wonder whether this was why he seemed to drop the ball just before each meeting.

Who knows?

They arranged to meet and go out for a drink. He was lovely and attentive and sent Tinderella little texts often, to remind her that he was thinking of her. The plan was to meet at a local bar to finally see each other in person. Tinderella, as she always did, had laid out the perfect outfit for their date. She had chosen a beautiful chiffon dress with an eye-catching floral design that suited the warm sunny weather, paired with her long brown boots. A pair of silver pendant earrings and her beautiful waterhole silver bracelet—ready to be her lucky charm—were sitting on her dresser, waiting to be worn.

Tinderella loved fashion, but that wasn't the only reason she dressed up for her dates. She made a point of caring for herself and putting her best self forward. She respected and believed in herself, and she wanted any potential partner to do so, too. The way she presented herself was a big part of that message

But, it was not to be. The lovely outfit wasn't going anywhere, and neither was Tinderella.

Ben messaged her, explaining he had taken a job in another city and was leaving town—immediately. Even after he apologised, Tinderella honestly thought she would never hear from him again.

But Ben maintained message contact, so they continued chatting and spoke often about making time to speak in person on the phone. The phone calls would just never eventuate. It was a challenge but neither of them could really put too much emotion into it. He was so far away, and Tinderella couldn't see how they would ever be able to meet in the middle, geographically or physically. Her life was busy! She was launching a new hair care range and had more and more business meetings interstate—in the opposite direction to where Ben was. Gradually, the calls and messages stopped.

Until, on a nice sunny day with the sky a bright shade of blue, Tinderella received a new message from Ben after weeks of silence. He was coming to town to visit his three kids, and he wanted to meet Tinderella in person while he was there. Her heart beat faster with excitement, but looking at her calendar, she found she had a clash in dates. Oh no! It fell on the same weekend as one of her best girlfriend's Christmas party.

Maya's annual, invite-only party was not to be missed. It was the event of the year—everyone looked forward to catching up at Maya's place. She was the perfect hostess and only invited the most amazing people. She was an events guru, and her Christmas party was always a hit!

Instead of trying to be in two places at once, Tinderella decided she would ask Maya if she could bring Ben along to the party as her plus-one. Maya was a person who welcomed everyone with open arms and had a genuine concern for the people she loved. She had a heart of pure gold. It was soon settled. Tinderella would bring Ben to Maya's 'party of the year' and it would all be great!

Who was she kidding?

Tinderella spent the first two hours of the party waiting for Ben's call. Her heart was torn in two. She wasn't able to give the party a chance! Waiting on Ben kept her distracted from her friends, and she had to stay sober because she had agreed to pick him up after he saw his kids.

When his call finally came, he was a very happy camper. Ben was drunk and declared his love for Tinderella, asking her how his 'wifey' was on such a great night?

What a dick!

But affairs of the heart are always the most complicated and while Tinderella was not impressed, she was invested.

She stayed in touch with him and, as you can probably predict, he let her down, again!

This time, Tinderella took Ben's behaviour personally. She wondered if she would ever find the right man for her… and in that moment she went from sad to mad.

And she let him know it!

The online messages flew hard and fast and she called him every name under the sun.

His response? Nothing! Not a word.

He unfriended her, deleted her number, blocked her. It was done.

Arsehole.

Tinderella had never been ghosted before.

Was it the end? Of course not!

Not too long afterward, she heard from him again. He was moving back to the city. He had missed his kids, and he needed to be closer to them.

Ben was back.

Yay, she thought, with little or no enthusiasm.

She still wasn't really sure how she felt about this faux relationship. There were so many question marks, but she was still single and not seeing anyone at the time, so... against her better judgment, she agreed to 'possibly' catch up once he was back in town.

Time passed, and she noticed she could see his profile on the dating sites again. Ben must have unblocked her. She connected with him again, and suddenly, he had news to tell her. He was in a budding relationship—an old school friend he had reconnected with online just that week. He said they'd been chatting for a bit and it had obviously blossomed into something more. Tinderella was sincerely happy for him, as she had forgiven his past actions and wished him well.

Ben went silent again. Time passed and Tinderella filed the whole experience under the 'past failures' tab of her dating experiences catalogue, until...

Yes, you guessed it. Ben reached out to Tinderella again. He started a new online chat thread, telling her that he still thought she was a very sexy woman. He still wanted to see her and have his way with her.

Well, the man certainly knew how to get her attention. Or maybe Tinderella was just a little goal-driven and now had some ego in the game—either way she felt compelled to respond. Ben then told her the old school friend he had been seeing had gone back to her husband... and actually asked Tinderella on a date!

Well this was progress, but Tinderella was a little apprehensive after her past experiences with him. Maybe it was actually going to happen after all these months? She was feeling really good about herself right then. She had lost the extra weight she had clung to over the past few years, and felt a new sense of happiness in her life as Tinderella—the single, sexy chick.

So she agreed to the date, and they arranged a time and place.

On the day of the big date, Tinderella contacted Ben to ask if they could meet a little later than he had asked as she still had more clients to see. She had learnt from past experiences to have her dates work around her, rather than to work around them. That way, she wasn't let down and inconvenienced. Welcome to dating in the modern world!

Tinderella pushed the time back two hours and was looking forward to his response of 'Of course, I'll see you then'. But, nope. Instead of the hoped-for response her brain had rehearsed throughout the day, she got, 'Sorry, but I've had to go interstate for a family matter. I'll have to postpone.'

Tinderella felt for him, because she knew it was always a challenge when you had to quickly rush off to help family. On the other hand, she wasn't surprised. Ben, the slippery one, had wriggled his way out of meeting her yet again.

Oh, for goodness sake, when will she ever learn?

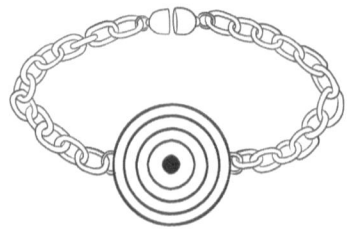

It's Time to Talk... by Simone

PUT YOUR BEST SELF FORWARD

Your online dating journey can be a journey of self-discovery. It is an opportune time to hold the mirror up to yourself. You're not just looking at the external beautiful you—whether you need a new hairstyle, a new wardrobe, new makeup, or a facial—but also the 'inside' you. Does your self-esteem need a boost? How much do you love who you are as a person? Do you need to set aside some time for yourself, just as much as you are setting aside time for dating? Do you have healthy boundaries and are you putting your own needs first? This is an important reminder to treat yourself as you want to be treated by others.

It's completely understandable if you're dealing with a range of issues that can affect body confidence and self-esteem generally. Many of us worry about how childbearing, age, illness and operations, accidents, or simply our modern, typically super-busy and stressed lifestyles can impact on a woman's face and body. We fret over wrinkles and stretch marks, scars and saggy bits, or unwanted extra weight. The important thing is to accept yourself for who you are, knowing the man you find on your journey, your soul mate, will adore you for who you are, for all you are, warts and all. Remember, you are the only you there has ever been, and that alone makes you amazing and beautiful—from the inside out.

Take a leaf from Tinderella's book and make a point of being kind and respectful to yourself. Give yourself the gift of time and attention and see how you shine.

DEALING WITH EGOS, EXPECTATIONS AND EXCUSES

Working out people's true intentions on a dating site can be a real challenge. Sometimes it's pretty obvious—there will be guys who make it clear that they are only after sex. Others *say* they are searching for love, but their actions don't align with their words and their behaviours can be inconsiderate, confusing or hurtful.

There are also those who are ego driven. They want to feel good purely by having multiple women show interest in them. The more matches, likes and kisses they get, the better. It is simply a numbers game to them.

Some guys will 'ghost' women—that is, they cut off all contact without any apparent warning or justification and ignore any attempts to reach out or communicate. There are many reasons for this behaviour, including losing interest, getting a kick out of hurting others, or being unable to deal with their own emotions after connecting with a woman online. Perhaps they're not emotionally ready for a relationship. It's selfish behaviour which may make you feel as if you've done something wrong. Rest assured, this is usually not the case, but is instead the action of a man who is rude, insensitive, spineless or all three.

Reasons why people let others down

There are many reasons why people consistently let others down, whether they're strangers, dates, or close family and friends. Any of the following reasons could explain Ben's behaviour:

- Values: we all have values we live by, even if we are not consciously aware of them. It's possible that dating was not high on Ben's hierarchy of values, even though he was on a dating site. His highest values may lie elsewhere, for example, his work, friends or family.
- Narcissist behaviour: when someone is dismissive of another person's time, it could be because they have narcissistic personality traits. This is because a narcissist views their own needs as more important than others' needs. They won't take your feelings and needs into consideration, even if they act in a way that lets you down or hurts you. Another narcissistic trait is the need to keep

people 'hanging' to prop up their own inflated sense of self.
- Lack of organisation skills: Yes, Ben could just be super disorganised. Some people who are disorganised like to think they have a laid back approach to life and believe they are much calmer for it. However, this view may not be shared by other people dealing with the impacts of Ben's approach.
- ADHD: people who have ADHD don't just lose track of time—they often don't know how to track it in the first place! They also become easily overwhelmed and exhausted from hyper focusing on the things they are interested in, to the detriment of everything else. They can overcommit to people, and often have to make changes at the last minute to keep their commitments to others.
- Depression: the symptoms of depression can sometimes be mistaken for a 'couldn't-be-fucked' attitude and a general disregard for other people's plans and expectations. In reality, one of the symptoms of depression is withdrawal from people, society, events and experiences.
- Low self-esteem and/or low confidence: it is possible Ben's profile photo wasn't an accurate reflection of how he appears in real life because he's not confident in how he looks now. Therefore, he didn't want to get caught out, particularly as Tinderella knew Ben's mutual friend.

You are in control

No matter the reason, agreeing to meet and then cancelling on a date with little notice, or just not showing up on multiple occasions, is inconsiderate and rude in anyone's books. We all understand plans can change at the last minute, but it would seem Ben is not ready (or willing) to commit to the process of dating, even though he gave the impression he wanted to date Tinderella.

It's important to remind yourself that you don't need to sit around and wait to connect with these 'slippery' guys. You can decide to date or not date a person. To date for sex, friendship or a committed relationship. To swipe right or left. To match with a guy, or not.

Courtesy and respect are just as important online as they are in real life. If your chosen guy can't act this way in the virtual world, be wary of his ability to follow through in the real world. Be clear on what you will and will not accept. Knowing you have choice is an important element of healthy self-esteem. When you take control of the process, you are unlikely to settle for less than you deserve.

LEARNINGS FROM TINDERELLA AND BEN

1. It's okay to make allowances for people who cancel at the last minute, if they encounter things outside their control. However, when your date is cancelling on you more often than not, then it's usually not just bad luck. It's more likely to be an indicator of other behaviours and intentions that ultimately indicate you are not high on their list of priorities.

2. There can be underlying causes for a person's slippery behaviour, particularly in the online dating world. On one end of the scale, a person who makes arrangements to meet up and then cancels at the last minute could be suffering from self-esteem issues or depression—or just laziness. On the other end of the scale, they could be ghosting you, or they are a narcissist.

3. The whole idea of online dating is to date! Yep—to actually meet up with people! You have to be prepared to meet at some point, so if the guy you're talking with online continually fobs you off, don't waste any more time on him. Move on to the next guy who will actually want to meet you.

Chapter 6

Mick

There is nothing either good or bad, but thinking makes it so.

- William Shakespeare

Tinderella's encounter with Mick was the closest she had come to *Fifty Shades of Grey* in her life. To this day it still made her smile and shake her head.

She had the Tinder app open on her iPhone, looking at the eligible men on Tinder, and came across Mick. He was a street artist, which she found quietly exciting. He was rugged and handsome in his pics, with a slight three-day growth and a whole lot of tattoos. Some girls like them, and some don't… Tinderella liked them!

She started to chat to him and instantly liked this guy. He was self-assured and honest to the point of being blunt. Straight as the day is long and very much to the point. He didn't hold back.

Mick was online to meet women to have sex with. That was it, just sex.

He loved sex. And he loved talking about it and doing it. All different ways—and he left nothing to the imagination in his messages. It sure sounded like this guy was very experienced and skilled in the art of sex. Tinderella was curious. He had her attention. She wanted to meet him in person and see if he was all that he was cracked up to be.

Tinderella was at it again, and this time she had a mission. She was going to learn about sex—things she'd never experienced before! She was intrigued and excited; like the innocent Anastasia Steele, she was about to go into another dimension, a parallel reality.

She dressed carefully for their first meeting, in black skinny jeans and a loose-fitting top that draped around her breasts and defined them. It was a soft, pale blue colour, and made her feel very pretty. She'd decided to use her waterfall bracelet as a locket. Pinned between her breasts, it also accentuated their shape. Long black boots amped up the sex appeal and helped get her into the mood. Hopefully, it was enough to seduce her date.

Tinderella still didn't know a lot about Mick when the Uber dropped her at his house. She had enjoyed a glass of wine while waiting for her ride and Mick was on the other side of a couple of Johnny Walkers, so he was tipsy too.

She was impressed by Mick's home, a well-furnished, two-storey brick house he shared with a flatmate. He led her straight upstairs to his bedroom. Tinderella was shocked to find the mattress was on the floor. Mick told her it was best for sex, without the bedframe. Giggling, she was taken aback, but also mildly curious.

She asked to use the bathroom. It was on the opposite side of the hall to his bedroom, and as she went in, she had to stifle a gasp. Sex toys lined the rim of the bathtub. She looked at it all, then back at Mick. With a smile, she said to him, 'Oh my, you are a deviant!' and shut the door.

Alone in the bathroom, she studied each piece.

There were thick yellow rubber gloves; mouth gags in four different sizes; nipple clamps; whips; and other toys of amusement. Is *all* of this his? she wondered. What had she walked into? Tinderella felt overwhelmed in this unfamiliar environment. Should she stay or should she go? She decided to stay. She felt safe and had become even more intrigued and curious....

Mick was waiting for her when she opened the bathroom door and he took her hand and led her into his bedroom. He'd lit candles, and they were arranged strategically around the room. Tinderella smiled, thinking how cute this was. He was obviously trying to help her feel relaxed and comfortable, while setting a mood for sex.

She sat down on his bed and he sat in front of her, looking deep into her eyes. She felt his confidence and started to feel a little shy, and in that moment, she had to look away.

Slowly, he reached for her left leg and held it whilst he started to unzip her long black boot and slid it off and placed it delicately to the side. He then held her right leg and did the same. Then Mick started to undress her, piece by piece, with deliberate care and focus. First her socks, then her top, and then he unbuttoned her jeans and pulled them down, one leg at a time. Finally, he slid his fingers behind her back and expertly undid her red lace bra and laid it neatly with her other clothing. He was well-rehearsed at this. Her full breasts were now on view and she felt very exposed. Mick stood and started to undress in front of her.

His body was very masculine and Tinderella watched him with great interest. Mick's physique was defined, and he had a fine dusting of chest hair that looked soft and not too thick. He had tattoos on his body, but the subdued lighting didn't allow her to see them clearly.

After removing all of his clothes, Mick leant down towards her and kissed her full on the lips. Tinderella's heart was beating quickly in her chest and she enjoyed this kiss, his tongue playing its own game in her mouth. Mick knew exactly how to kiss. This man was an artful lover, and she was ready to be with him.

They lay on the bed together and he began to explore her body, running his hands up and down. Soon he was making her body react to his touch and take on its own agenda. Tinderella's back began to arch and her breathing came faster. His fingers stopped on her left breast, playing with her nipple. It rose up, erect. Her body was out of her control and under his, and Tinderella had to just go with what was happening in the moment. Again, he began to kiss her passionately on the lips and this time she kissed him back with a newfound passion.

He stayed close to her, looking into her eyes, and whispered, 'Have you ever had the belt?'

Tinderella had no idea what he was asking her. Did he want to beat her with a belt? What had she gotten herself into here? With some concern, Tinderella asked him, 'Do you want to beat me?'

He laughed. 'Of course not, Tinderella. I am a Dominant. I am not into punishing for my sexual pleasure. I use my selection of tools to do things that increase sexual pleasure for both of us. I take my sex partner to the brink of sexual excitement, so they can explode with the ultimate orgasm. I'll show you,' he said.

And he reached for a leather belt. He asked her to turn over and kneel on his bed. She did as he asked, and he gently guided her to lean forward and use her arms to support herself. Then he was behind her and touching her butt, running his hand over the most private parts of her body. He strapped the belt around her waist and tightened it to be firm, but not too tight. He explained he was going to use it as leverage and he was going to enter her from behind.

Okay, Tinderella, get a grip—pardon the pun! What the heck was going on here? What are you doing right now? She could hear the voices in her head, but it was too late to protest.

She felt his manhood enter her. He gently pulled back on the belt and she felt him enter her deep and hard. She had never been with a man who had used a belt to hold her during sex. It was a very different experience and her body responded with raw sexual desire, accepting his manhood fully.

Mick changed position until he was on top and penetrated her again. She began to actively participate. Tinderella wanted to share this experience and felt she needed to take back some of the control in this moment.

Big mistake!

Mick's body started to shift, and he began to move awkwardly. Tinderella could sense his discomfort, and how the sexual vibe began to change as Mick struggled with her newfound dominance. His manhood started to deflate, and he physically had to pull away. Tinderella was so confused. What had just happened?

She looked at him with concern. He was showing signs of embarrassment and his once hard erection had disappeared, leaving his cock limp and unresponsive.

Mick rolled away, telling her he couldn't finish. He was so shocked; it was clear this was not something he was used to. He really didn't know how to deal with the situation and wondered whether maybe he had drunk too much, so that his body was not responding in the way he needed it to. He explained he wasn't able to be with another dominant in the bedroom. It wasn't what gave him his sexual desire and excitement.

So, wow! Am I, Tinderella, a Domme too? she asked herself.

She had never even considered she liked to be dominant in bed, but after he explained, she realised that, at times, she did! She certainly liked to have a significant part in the bedroom and needed to feel she was part of the whole process. But did that mean she was a dominatrix?

Mick explained he needed a completely submissive partner.

And this wasn't her.

Tinderella reassured him it was okay, and she didn't take it personally. This was just life! Even with her reassurances, he continued to be regretful and apologise.

Mick left the room to allow her to get dressed. She met him outside in the hallway, and they chatted about what had just happened. They were both adults and knew that sometimes things happened that were out of their control. He was a nice guy, and Tinderella even felt a little sorry for him. She decided to ask him about the sex equipment she had seen earlier.

He led her into the bathroom and began to talk her through each piece of equipment and explained their uses. He came to the nipple clamps and asked if she wanted to feel them on. Yes, she wanted to know, so she allowed him to clip them onto her nipples. Oh, they pinched! It was a feeling that was both sensual and painful. Mick laughed at her response and removed them, telling her they were designed to do just that, to give the feeling of painful pleasure. Interesting... She had not been exposed to this before and she felt like a student, soaking up all the information she was hearing.

Together, they went downstairs to sit outside. They talked and had a drink, ending the day with a few giggles about what had just happened. Nothing helped heal an awkward situation like a drink over casual chitchat. During their conversation, Mick mentioned there was an event for the sexually free coming up, and he invited Tinderella to come along to the invite-only do. He told her if she were to attend, she would witness things she had never seen before. This was the wild side of sexual fantasies and she would have to have an open mind. Mick said there would be people there with every fetish, participating in every sexual act known to man. It would be an eye-opener for her, and he promised to find her a 'submissive' whilst she was there.

Although the offer was very kind and sincere, and she could tell that he wanted her to feel happy and find someone who suited her sexual chemistry, she declined politely and, on that note, Tinderella thought it was time to go. Mick walked her to his front door and kissed her kindly on the cheek, and she climbed into her second Uber of the night.

Tinderella left with newfound knowledge, smiling as she thought about how different we all are as individuals. She could accept that, without any judgment towards anyone. She wished Mick well in his search for a new sexual partner. She felt she had grown a little with the knowledge she now had, and with that, Tinderella closed the book on that chapter.

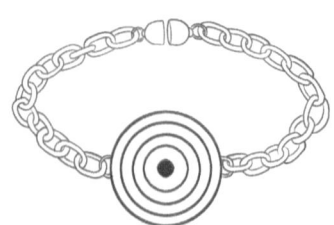

It's Time to Talk… by Simone

DATING FOR SEXUAL DISCOVERY

Returning to the dating game after many years in a relationship can often include a journey of sexual discovery. Dating different guys provides opportunities to learn more about the pleasures of the flesh.

Younger women coming of age in the twenty-first century may be sexually free, confident and experienced. Many of us whose primary relationships began last century may only have had sex with our long-term partner. For those with little experience—or a lack of recent experience—with bedding another man, the mere thought of sex with a new partner post-divorce or separation can be fraught with a combination of nervousness and curiosity. It can also be wildly exciting, or anything in between.

The good news is self-discovery can be very empowering for women. Exploring your needs and desires in the bedroom can provide a newfound confidence. All women should be free to express their preferences, and to explore as fully as they wish their sexual persuasion, fantasies and fetishes.

LEARN AS YOU GO

I know through my therapy practice, speaking with professional colleagues, and conversations amongst my own circle of friends, it is a fact that many women have never experienced an orgasm during their marriage. It's possible for women to *think* they had experienced orgasms with their ex-partners, but after being with new lovers, they realise this actually wasn't the case.

For the first time in their adult lives, the dating journey provides many women the means to truly explore and enjoy learning about how their bodies respond to skilled sexual touch. Being with an experienced partner who wants to please her can bring a woman to heights of orgasm she may have never experienced before.

Sexual self-discovery can be incredibly daunting. Thankfully, extensive information is available to enlighten and entertain the masses about all things sex! Movies, books, websites, sex shops and sex expos offer opportunities for educating and satisfying the curious mind. If you are unsure about anything to do with anatomy, sexual positions, fetishes, fantasies, squirting, masturbation or any other aspect of sexuality you can always Google it! Of course, nothing compares with experiencing things firsthand and learning as you go.

MANAGE YOUR EXPECTATIONS

Remember not all women (or men) use online dating sites and apps for the sole purpose of finding a life partner. Today it is far more acceptable and even expected for people to use online dating apps to fulfil their sexual needs and explore sexual desires and fantasies.

Feeling horny can be a great motivator for an online 'hook-up' with no strings attached, or as an alternative to solo masturbation. If you feel like doing this, I guarantee there will always be guys ready and willing to help satisfy a woman's sexual urges. There is no shame in doing this! Consider yourself an independent 'free agent'. You have the freedom to pursue your own sexual pleasures—without judgement! It is your body, your mind, and you have the choice to do whatever gives you joy... and pleasure.

There are also avenues to explore your sexuality through online communities, such as dating apps for threesomes and swingers. You can sign up with a fake name to protect your identity... and then go experimenting! Options include:

- Feeld – for open-minded couples and singles
- 3somer – for kinky, open-minded couples and singles who want to find 3-some relationships
- KinkD – to find and establish a kinky relationship with like-minded people.

AN INTRODUCTION TO BDSM

The massive success of the *Fifty Shades of Grey* book series indicates there is a demand for women seeking sexual enlightenment and erotic experiences, and an increasing curiosity about BDSM.

For the uninitiated, the umbrella term BDSM includes bondage and discipline (B&D), dominance and submission (D&S), and sadism and masochism (S&M) These are described as follows:

Bondage and discipline

When one partner physically restrains the other person to inflict pain, pleasure or humiliation. The person being bound and the person conducting the discipline both achieve sexual arousal through their actions. This is a consensual activity and requires the use of a safe word. Types of bondage include ropes, chains, handcuffs or blindfolds to restrict movement and heighten the senses. The bonding can involve parts of the body, e.g. hands or feet spread apart, or the entire body, e.g. hanging from a swing, fully bound in a rubber suit. The infliction of 'punishment' by the disciplinarian, such as withholding orgasms, whipping, acts of humiliation, e.g. forcing oral sex be performed, is said to be highly arousing for both parties.

Dominance and submission

Focuses on role-playing and power in an erotic context. One partner takes on the role of 'dominant' (sometimes called the top, or the Master), and the other takes on the role of the 'submissive' (also called the bottom). The primary role of the submissive is to pleasure the dominant sexually and the role of the dominant is to demand the submissive to sexually pleasure themselves, or the dominant. This role-playing can be switched between parties and can sometimes extend beyond the bedroom into their everyday lives.

Sadism and Masochism

S&M involves pain—both inflicting it (sadism) and receiving it (masochism)—to become sexually aroused or to achieve an orgasm. The types of pain inflicted include biting, spanking, whipping and genital torture, as well as psychological humiliation. S&M is more about the control one person has over another and can involve extreme forms of pain.

Don't be afraid to research this topic. There are many books that can provide an accurate (and arousing) overview of BDSM. Amazon has thousands of novels, volumes of short stories, handbooks and guides on BDSM. Online sex video sites also include countless videos of people partaking in BDSM which are informative and educational as well as arousing. Remember, as with any lifestyle choice, there are extreme forms of all aspects of BDSM, which can be shocking to the first-time viewer. It is not a one size fits all practice. Educate yourself and discover what might work for you!

Women who are into one form or another of BDSM say they really love it. Being a sub to a man's Dom can be erotically exciting. For example, a Dom may send a text messages to his sub at work, ordering her to masturbate in a toilet cubicle, or to sit at her desk and think about sex with her man until she becomes highly aroused—but not to 'release' herself until she is permitted to do so by her lover when she arrives home to him.

There are BDSM dungeons and clubs in every capital city in the world. These are easily found after a few clicks on any search engine. If you type in BDSM into Facebook, you'll see plenty of BDSM online groups you could join. As a member, you'll then find out the locations of clubs and events near you. Guests are welcome to attend BDSM clubs to explore the lifestyle, although privacy provisions must be respected and strictly adhered to. Who knows, you may see your boss or a school mum you know at one of these clubs.

Consent and Safety

BDSM practises are <u>always</u> consensual and should not be confused with unsolicited/criminal acts of sexual violence. People who enjoy BDSM usually negotiate and plan out their role playing adventures within the confines of their own personal levels of comfort and well-communicated boundaries. When it comes to BDSM, there is

always consent and a safe word that is pre-determined before any role-playing begins.

With Mick, Tinderella experienced a situation where her date was playing the role of a Dominant, with the assumption that Tinderella would play the role of a submissive. What was clearly missing in this situation was agreement from Tinderella about her role in this fantasy. Perhaps Mick thought the sex toys on display were the unspoken invitation to this live action play for two. Unfortunately for Mick, his poor communication and direction meant the play was a flop (pun intended.)

BEWARE SEXTING

We've all read the stories of celebrities who have had their naked photos shared by ex-boyfriends. Remember, anything posted or transmitted online lasts forever. It should always be your choice to take pictures of your body to share with someone. Do so with the understanding that any photos you share of yourself with a guy may not be deleted when you delete him out of your life.

It is also your choice to decide not to take photos to share with a guy. You may encounter pressure to send nude or partially nude photos, or to reciprocate when a man sends through his nude pics (whether you asked for them). If you don't feel comfortable taking naked photos of yourself, then don't! Seriously, if a guy needs to see you naked to converse with you online, then is he really worth getting to know on a deeper level?

The same goes for sexting, i.e. having sexually explicit and suggestive conversations via text or online messages.

No matter what—to sext or not to sext is totally up to you! If you enjoy it, then text away. It can be a huge turn-on and create amazing sexual tension in the lead-up to meeting a guy you like. But if engaging in sexually explicit and creative conversations is not your cup of tea, then don't. It may be something the two of you engage in after you've met, or had sex, but until you're ready, don't succumb to going there with him if you're not comfortable. It's not a pre-requisite to dating a guy.

There's also no way to avoid being sent unsolicited dick pics from time to time. Some men delight in sharing pictures of their appendages with unsuspecting women. These men may sometimes get the response they desire, but more often than not, their profiles are quickly deleted by shocked and angered women. If you are genuinely enjoying an online conversation with a guy who then sends you an unsolicited dick pic, you may wish to share with him your disappointment at his assumption you would find such a photo appealing. Or you could just end the conversation. Don't feel bad, or think he's done this because you've led him on. These guys are usually either 'players' or are insecure and feel women would only like them because of their bodies.

Some guys will heap abuse on women who won't engage with them via sexting, so please don't think it's just you, and don't engage. These sorts of stories are plentiful amongst women using online dating sites. Be reassured such men are in the minority. There are plenty of really nice guys out there who would be horrified to know others of their gender behave so badly.

ANOTHER REMINDER ABOUT SAFE SEX!

Ladies, a gentle reminder to get yourself checked for STIs before you begin your search for a soul mate. Stay healthy and always use a condom for protection. Condoms are also a reliable form of contraception when they are used correctly. If the guy says he'll withdraw so as not to get you pregnant, then he clearly doesn't understand how his body's reproduction system works, as sperm can be released with pre-cum fluid prior to ejaculation. There are also condoms for women, which are loose-fitting pouches designed to be inserted into the vagina. These female condoms have a ring at the top to hold it in place outside the vagina. You can also use condoms on vibrators and sex toys. Other forms of protection against STIs include latex products such as dental dams (square pieces of latex that cover your vagina during oral sex) and gloves the guy wears when he's fingering you.

If you'd like more advice and guidance on safe sex, contact your nearest Family Planning or Sexual Health Centre. Your doctor will also have appropriate and helpful advice and contacts for similar services.

LEARNINGS FROM TINDERELLA AND MICK

1. Always use condoms.

2. Dating after many years in a relationship is often a time when women truly open themselves up to the infinite possibilities of self-expression through multiple sexual experiences. Be open to this—and enjoy the experience of sexual discovery!

3. BDSM is no longer taboo. Research this topic and decide for yourself if this is for you. If you'd like to explore BDSM with your date, ensure you always use a safe word so he knows when you need to pause, change positions or stop the experience altogether. When things get heated and bodies become aroused it is easy to run with the role play and get lost in pleasure, but it's okay to pull back or stop at any time if you're not feeling comfortable.

Chapter 7

Baz

The real lover is the man who can thrill you just by touching your head or smiling into your eyes—or just by staring into space.

- Marilyn Monroe

Baz was a work of art in every way.

His body was a full canvas of his life story, with tigers and panthers amongst the African designs. He stood tall, 130 kilograms of pure muscle. Tinderella saw his profile online and couldn't swipe right fast enough.

He had a bad boy look about him and was very easy on the eyes. They soon connected and were discovering everything there was to know about each other. Baz had moved to Australia from South Africa and he had just been released from prison.

Tinderella can guess what you are thinking—abort, abort!

Wise advice. However, in usual Tinderella style, she didn't.

Instead, she was curious, wanting to know what had happened, and Baz told her his story. She heard him out, and she believed him.

He had been convicted of aggravated assault causing grievous bodily harm against a man who had attacked, raped and beaten his daughter's close friend. The rapist had inflicted immeasurable harm to this girl, leaving her emotionally broken and too anxious to leave the security of her own home. Baz's protective instincts took over, and he responded by tracking the perpetrator down. When he found him, he put him in the boot of his car, drove to an abandoned building, gave him a 'touch-up' and threw him off the building, watching as he hit the ground.

The rapist survived and Baz was given four years in jail.

It was his fifth time in jail, and his last. After serving the time, he decided to start a new life in Australia, and was accepted without objection into the country.

To be fair, had Tinderella known how much jail time he had served when they first connected online, she may have not agreed to their initial meeting. Once she met him, it couldn't be ignored. He had four dots tattooed in a line on the right side of his face to show time served, something she hadn't noticed in his profile pics. The fifth tattoo was larger, signifying the difference in the crime from the earlier convictions.

Baz intrigued her, and they got to know each other as they shared their stories. Baz had been in relationships in the past, and he told her how his heart had been broken many times, leaving him with deep feelings of abandonment.

He had been a bouncer in South Africa, and he was well known on the club circuit back in his birth country. As an experienced street fighter, he had been very popular for his ability to diffuse a situation quickly. They rarely challenged him when he stepped in, and he took control swiftly. He told her was connected with the gangs but had never sworn his allegiance to anyone in particular. This meant he was well respected and accepted by all. It was evident he could stand on his own two feet.

For some reason, Tinderella was not scared or fazed by this history. She was not a judgmental person and believed everyone deserved a second chance. Make no mistake, the little Tinderella voice in her told her to be mindful and cautious where needed. She never needed to be. Despite his rough history and fighting ability, Tinderella became the dominant one in this relationship. Baz respected that she hadn't judged him for his past and he never once hurt her or raised a hand to her or said a harsh word.

Baz had returned to the club scene and was working at a local pub as part of the security crew, a job he was confident in and found fulfilling. He was naturally very strong and didn't believe in steroids or artificial stimulants. His food habits were incredibly disciplined, and he drank up to eight litres water a day. He spent four to five hours in the gym every day to build up his body and was very proud of his achievements. He did look good, and often had women solicit him to go to bed.

For all these reasons and more, he was appealing to the opposite sex and, although he was quite shy, he knew what women wanted.

The online relationship soon blossomed into more messages via social media, texts or talks on the phone. They finally agreed to meet…

They chose a date, but the trouble was he lived at least three hours away from her, so Tinderella had to decide whether to drive all that way to see him. She had to weigh up the pros and cons and think about the situation. She decided to go. She wanted to see him and see if there was chemistry between them.

We all know there is wisdom in hindsight. Looking back, Tinderella could see it was a total mismatch, and it would never work. At the time she had her blinkers on and she couldn't see the whole picture clearly.

The day came, and she headed to the coast. Three hours gives a person a long time to think and turn around to head home… but no, Tinderella kept driving. She arrived at the hotel she had booked into for the two days away in what felt like no time.

She messaged Baz to tell him she had arrived.

Tinderella was on another adventure! What else was a girl to do, to find love? Oh, okay—we all know it was really lust!

Tinderella booked into the hotel and unpacked all of her things. She had brought food, nibbles and everything she needed for the weekend. Yes, she was staying overnight. She settled into the room, poured herself a glass of wine and turned the television on.

Before long there was a quiet knock on the door. It was Baz. She opened the door and this large confident man walked into the room. He looked like an African version of Thor.

He was divine.

He came close to her and kissed her on the cheek. He held her with one hand on her back—it was lovely, and she felt very comfortable in the moment.

She had dressed in a short navy skirt, a tight halter top, and red heels. She looked a little nautical to be honest, but she had travelled to meet at the seaside, so it seemed suited to the occasion. Her trusty waterhole bracelet provided the finishing touch to her cheeky little outfit.

Baz took a step back to take in the woman before him, and he couldn't help but tell Tinderella how beautiful she was. 'Fucking gorgeous,' to be exact.

She felt the same about him. She started to get a little flustered, but he soon put her mind at ease when he took her hand and led her across to the bed. Baz sat down and pulled her onto the bed. He laid her next to him and held her. It was so sweet.

He told her how nice it was that she had driven so far to see him. He was excited she was there, next to him. Tinderella could feel his body warmth and it was oh, so very nice! He tilted her head up to his, to have their lips close... so close. She could feel his breath on her lips and it was gentle and reassuring. Then he kissed her.

It was warm, soft and long. It was beautiful. He was a fabulous kisser and Tinderella enjoyed the feeling of his tongue searching for hers inside her mouth. Ahhhh... to do this correctly, the guy needs the right amount of experience and he has to be able to use his tongue in the right way—not too hard and not too soft, not too deep, and just deep enough.

His kiss was a true art form and she could feel her heart beat just a little faster. She was getting so turned on by him' she was putty in his hands.

Baz started to take her clothes off as he ran his hands, his tongue and his soft lips all over her exposed body parts. Before their meeting, Baz had spent about an hour shaving his whole body for her. He was smooth all over and every one of his muscles was defined on his beautifully structured body.

Tinderella's hands began to pull off his shirt; it was a tight fit on his masculine frame, so she had to bunch her hands in it on either side and pull it over his head. His scalp was shaven too, and he tilted his head forward so she could pull the shirt off him.

She ran her hands over his bare chest. It was indeed a work of art. Both of his nipples were pierced, and she played with the little metal balls on the end of each sleeper. Baz winced with delight, becoming more aroused with her touch. He ran his hands along her body and lifted her leg high, bringing her close against him. He was larger than she thought, and she could feel every inch of him as he entered her, their bodies becoming one.

The sex was extraordinary. This man could recover and reach orgasm time and time again... six times in fact. Tinderella lost track of time. Her body and mind belonged to him for hours. But it had to finish, as he had to go to his night job.

After such a long workout, Baz was hungry and needed to eat before going to work. He noticed the bananas Tinderella had purchased and brought them over to the bed. With a seductive look on his face he guided her legs open then broke off the banana and slowly ate the first piece. The whole time he was looking into her eyes with an expression of mischief and lust. When it came to the second piece, he broke it off and inserted into her opening and started to use it like a sexual tool. Tinderella was frozen in pleasure and shock! After what seemed like an eternity, he removed it and ate the piece of banana.

He repeated this several times until all the bananas were gone. As you may have guessed, Baz wasn't shy about introducing Tinderella to the things he wanted to do to her, and his member was still very hard. He was almost like a mythical creature... she couldn't explain the sexual energy he had. She had never experienced such variety in her sex life—the different positions, his ability to pick her up like a rag doll and place her gently on his manhood.

He was in total control.

Baz led her to the shower and washed her entire body, maintaining intense eye contact. She suddenly felt shy and insecure. Then his strong hands lifted her once more, and he directed himself inside her. His manhood reflected his body size and she could feel it penetrate her deeply. She began to orgasm with an intenseness she had never felt before.

When they finished, he rinsed her in a delicate and caring way, and pulled the towel around her clean body. He picked her up and carried her to the bed, laying her on her stomach. He oiled her all over, massaging her body. His experienced hands moved over her and her back arched in pleasure, responding to his touch, lifting and pointing her buttocks toward him.

Then he had to go.

Baz kissed her goodbye with a passion so intense, and his fingers were inside her again, finding her wetness and pleasuring her one last time. She was breathless and reached the height of ecstasy quickly.

It was an experience that Tinderella will take with her forever.

They were never to meet again. The distance between them just made it too difficult to keep any kind of relationship going.

It was like a fairytale.

It had a beginning and an end… with an exotic adventure in between.

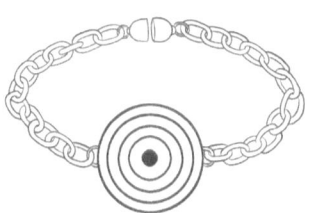

It's Time to Talk... by Simone

THE JOY OF SEX

As Mae West says, 'too much of a good thing can be wonderful'. Tinderella had exactly this experience with Baz. West, an American actress and a truly sexually liberated woman, was renowned for her appetite for gorgeous men. She had a breezy wit that left its mark and once said 'sex is emotion in motion'. Like West, most women would gladly welcome the chance to be in the arms of a hunky man with a desire to please them—again and again! Whether you're looking for booty calls, hook ups, casual dates, or a friends-with-benefits arrangement, there are plenty of opportunities in the land of online dating for no-strings-attached sex. How wonderful to explore this opportunity with a gorgeous male specimen.

At the core of Tinderella's experience with Baz was the deep respect he has for women. It is evident in the way he prepared himself physically for her (shaving his whole body), to the compliments he gave her, and the way he cared for her before, during and after their lovemaking. This man was strong and passionate, but also gentle and caring. Many of us love a man who takes the initiative in the bedroom. Add some gentleness, sensuality, intimacy and a desire to please and be pleasured, and you have a fabulous recipe for memorable and enjoyable sex.

A woman may find it challenging to be with a man who wants to pleasure her, particularly if she has been more focused on pleasuring her partner for many years instead of herself, or if she has had painful sexual experiences in the past. Being able to receive pleasure in the bedroom requires her to allow herself to feel vulnerable and open to receiving such pleasure. There is an element of trust required on her part for this experience, but with a guy who only wants her to orgasm, over and over again, sex can be a truly beautiful thing. Sex is at its most joyful when each person is fully open to the experience, respectful of their partner, and generous in their actions.

Interestingly, many women find it hard to receive love (above and beyond pleasure), even though they crave it. This can be due to an often unconscious fear of being loved unconditionally. We link this fear to feelings of lack of self-worth, or lack of a sense of being deserving enough, worthy enough, for such joy. If you can relate to this, then becoming aware of these feelings and patterns is the first step in healing to receive love—especially in the bedroom. It's worth holding the mirror up to yourself!

THE NEED FOR A HERO

Baz also has a protective nature, evident in his role as a bouncer, protecting club-goers from harm, and his willingness to avenge a heinous crime committed against a friend of his family. Women tend to be drawn to men who are protective, probably a genetic holdover from primitive times when men hunted, and women stayed close to home with the children. This may be why women are drawn to men in uniform. Not only are policemen, fireman, ambulance officers and military personnel protectors of our communities, but they usually take pride in keeping fit to be effective at their jobs. Protectiveness + fabulous physique + uniform = hugely attractive men! A healthy intimate relationship allows both you and your partner to feel supported and cared for when you need it. Knowing you have a 'safe place to fall' is a wonderful thing.

Not all 'bad boys' are bad men

The fact Baz had been to jail was not an issue for Tinderella because she got to know him as a person, and it was clear to her that despite his past convictions this man was kind—a good man. Not all men who go to jail are bad—they have just made bad choices. On release, many find it difficult to assimilate back into society because others tend to judge them on their past wrongs and discriminate against them.

Tinderella's story reminds us that when a person has served their time in jail, they have the right to be allowed to live their life without further judgement and become (or return to being) contributing members of society. How wonderful Tinderella could accept this man for who he was as a person and as a result, she enjoyed a most memorable time with him.

LEARNINGS FROM TINDERELLA AND BAZ:

1. Look for a lover that respects women, is generous in his lovemaking, and makes you feel safe. Trust your intuition.

2. It's a beautiful thing to receive pleasure from a generous lover. Being open-minded means you are likely to meet more men and have more experiences that expand your sexual fulfilment.

3. Everyone has a past and sometimes we make decisions we regret, but this shouldn't define us. This includes people who have been incarcerated, as they are entitled to enjoy life to the fullest upon release.

Chapter 8

Brad

Better a thousand times careful than once dead.
- Proverb

In her early days of dating, Tinderella's curiosity often drove her to put her own safety at risk. Thankfully, she had a good friend in Eliza, who gave her sound advice when it came to meeting new people through social media and taking care of her personal safety. She was very glad she could rely on this advice on the night she met Brad the knife maker, even if it was a case of 'better late than never'.

Meeting up with him was spontaneous, so Tinderella had put very little thought for her safety into this get-together. At Brad's suggestion, they met up on a weeknight on his side of town, an unfamiliar area for her. Tinderella saw him standing next to his car as she arrived in the car park and was a little surprised. He didn't look a lot like his images on the dating site and his car was old and beaten up.

Possibly, Tinderella should have walked away there and then, but no. True to character, she was an optimistic risk-taker. She pushed her initial misgivings aside and walked over to meet him. Brad seemed polite, and they walked to their chosen meeting place. When they discovered it was unexpectedly closed, Brad suggested they go back to his house around the corner to have a drink.

Oh, Tinderella... what are you getting into here? she asked herself.

Eliza's advice started to pass through her mind, but she pushed that away, too. She chose to go along with Brad to his house, although she followed him in her own car. That was her saving grace—her car gave Tinderella the security to make a quick getaway if she needed to.

They arrived at his home after a three-minute drive. It was a big, single storey house in a built-up area with neighbours close by. This put Tinderella's mind at ease a bit. Brad led her through his house, telling her to follow him to the man cave. It was huge, and looked more like a workshop, with several large commercial-style metal cabinets and other massive pieces of equipment lining the benches around two of the walls. Tinderella assumed he was a cabinetmaker or dabbled in woodwork. Oh, how wrong she was!

He indicated the pool table in the centre of the massive room with a small smile on his face, and suggested they play a game of strip pool, but offered to get her a drink first. Brad went to a custom-made bar he had designed to fit perfectly in one corner and fixed Tinderella a glass of champagne.

He talked as he poured, and Tinderella found out that Brad was a bladesmith. He had rods and panels of steel and metal all over the workshop and he explained the metal storage cabinets were full of custom-made knives, swords and special tools that needed to be stored under lock and key.

Who was this guy? She didn't know him from a bar of soap, yet here she was in his house, standing there in the workshop, surrounded by an extensive supply of blades and sharp equipment. Tinderella was hoping he didn't have a screw loose, but all she had was positive thinking—she had to believe she would be okay.

To his credit, Brad had remembered Tinderella liked to drink champagne and had it ready and nicely chilled. He passed the glass to her. It was unwashed, with a lipstick mark on the rim and she found it difficult to find a clean area to drink from, even after wiping it. She wondered if this was an indicator of the way he approached his relationships. Was this what he was used to?

Ohhhh, Tinderella!!! This isn't the guy! Listen to your inner voice!

Brad suggested they move to the couch next to the bar. Tinderella could hardly find a spot to sit as there were cushions and clutter everywhere. She had to shuffle a few things around to find a clean and safe area to sit.

By this stage, Tinderella was already mentally out the door, and she was thinking of ways she could leave without making too much fuss. A golden opportunity presented itself when Brad excused himself to go to the bathroom. Tinderella snatched up her phone and texted Eliza, begging her to call in the next few minutes and get her out of there!

Brad returned and sat next to her, then started telling her about his turbulent relationship with his ex-wife. The story seemed to go on and on. Tinderella was getting bored. She wasn't a psychologist—she was meant to be on a date! And now she was silently sending out mental SOSs to Eliza.

Ring now! Pleeeease, ring now!

Brad's story was one of complete betrayal, from his perspective at least. His ex had ruined him financially by running up huge debts on personal credit cards and hiding the financial disaster from him. It was obvious it had taken its toll.

This confessional was not a situation Tinderella wanted to be in, and she was a bit frustrated with his verbal attacks on his ex. If this was such a big thing in his life, why didn't he tell her about it when they were chatting previously? Why dump this all on her now? She slowly sipped the champagne, her mind drifting, thinking about other things. She was snapped back to reality when her phone rang. She quickly apologised to Brad and answered it. It was one of the best phone calls she had received in her life. It was her beautiful girlfriend, pretending to be one of her children. She didn't know whether to look concerned or burst out laughing at Eliza's creativity. After a minute on the phone, Tinderella apologised to Brad again, saying it was a family emergency, and she had to go as her children needed her.

Brad accepted the story, and she was up on her feet, ready to leave. She was so relieved that he didn't try to kiss her as she said her goodbyes or ask her for another date. She was out of there quicker than a hot knife through butter.

Pardon the pun.

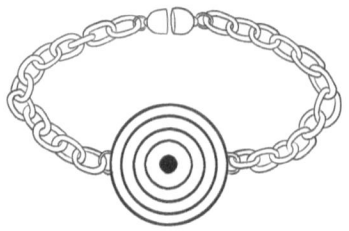

It's Time to Talk… by Simone

ALWAYS PLAN FOR YOUR OWN SAFETY

Those of us starting back in the dating game can sometimes be naïve to the dangers prevalent in society. Perhaps especially so if we have most recently been in a long-term relationship with a much-loved partner, and/or are still surrounded by trusted male relatives, colleagues and friends, as this can create a false sense of security. Yet stranger danger is as relevant to an adult as it is to a child, and it's best to take sensible precautions.

Meet first in a public place

It is always best to meet a guy for the first time in a 'safe' environment. A safe environment is a public place such as a bar, café, park or other well-patronised outdoor venue, a movie cinema, tourist site, cultural centre and so on. Check out any proposed venue if you are not familiar with it. Look up its opening hours online. Assess its general location and parking or public transport availability so you don't get caught out.

If there is chemistry worth exploring with the guy you've just met, then you can always arrange to meet again, where you feel comfortable. If you decide to go to his home, send a quick text to a girlfriend to let her know where you're going. Include his address and a screenshot of his profile photo and consider adding a time when you'll check in with your friend to let her know you're okay.

When it comes to it, if you don't feel comfortable with the proposed arrangements on where to meet, ask to change them. Or ultimately, cancel the date altogether if the guy, or the place he wants to meet, seems dodgy.

Even in a country as well-policed and law-abiding as Australia, there are still the few bad apples who need to be avoided. In an ideal world, violence against women would not exist, but until we achieve that, you mustn't ignore your safety.

Do your due diligence

Pay attention when you meet new men on dates. Remember, a person's true self is often not revealed for months or even years into a relationship. Since the late seventeenth century when the first 'personals' ad was placed in a British agricultural journal, there have been those willing to prey on trusting hopefuls seeking love. Our superconnected digital world gives scammers and fraudsters the perfect playground. Happily, it's not common, but it is common enough to include here as part of your online dating preparation.

It is essential to do your due diligence before agreeing to meet with any new man. This can be as simple as a Google search on his name, and checking other online sources such as Facebook, LinkedIn and Instagram. Cross-reference the information you find and see if you can verify any claims he is making about himself.

Trust your instincts

Tinderella's story also serves as a reminder to trust your instincts. Your mind is like a radar and receives more information than you consciously know. The way your mind communicates with you is via 'gut feelings' or your intuition. You may not be sure about what is causing you to feel uncomfortable in a certain situation. Listen to your instincts and do a mental scan to determine what may be amiss. And then act on it!

HOME IS WHERE THE HEART IS

The state of a person's home should not be ignored when considering a guy's potential to become your life partner, particularly if cleanliness and organised living are high on your list of values. Your home is your sanctuary, a safe place inside, to which you can retreat from the busy, crazy outside world. If a person's home is terribly cluttered and unclean, every corner and surface covered with stuff and worse, it's likely to indicate something more is going on than just being a little short on time to manage the cleaning that week. When 'inside' is as scary as 'outside', this can lead to feelings of hopelessness and anxiety.

To be fair, there are many levels of 'clean and tidy', and some people are very comfortable in spaces considered disorganised, messy and chaotic by most others. Where some might see only the chaos, these people will describe it as 'organised chaos'. This is not uncommon in people who are creative; people who have ADHD; or teenagers. Others of us including parents of young children; people who are time poor; and people who have too much on their plate, to name but a few, adapt our standards to our circumstances.

Living in filth is another thing altogether and is often accompanied by a lack of conscious awareness and/or a lack of desire to clean. It can indicate depression or low self-respect, or a possible disregard for others' comfort and wellbeing—something that may be problematic if you wish your lover to practice safe sex. Squalor in a person's home is incredibly off-putting, as experienced by Tinderella at Brad's house. It's one thing when someone drops in unannounced and you've been putting off cleaning for a while, but I think we all understand how Tinderella felt when Brad handed her a dirty glass.

Everyone has the right to be messy and even unclean at times in their own home. However, if you are looking for a life partner who has similar values around house and home, then you are likely going to be put off by your new date's lack of cleanliness. If you really like a guy who places a low priority on keeping a house clean and presentable, ask yourself if you feel comfortable taking on the role of a nagging, controlling perfectionist, because you'll likely be called that often in the future when you clash with your messy, untidy partner.

IS YOUR DATE READY TO DATE?

Tinderella was very uncomfortable when Brad spoke at length of the hurt, pain and anger he felt at the actions of his ex-wife. This is not an uncommon experience to encounter when you start dating. Most people are on dating sites because they are genuinely seeking connection—whether it is through sex, friendship or a relationship. Some will have had horrendous experiences with their ex-partners. They are not just lonely and in pain, they still have a lot of anger towards the ex and are wanting to fill that void and forget the pain and anger through dating or having sex. They may want to talk about these experiences with you as part of their processing of these events and emotions, but this is not your responsibility.

LEARNINGS FROM TINDERELLA AND BRAD:

1. Your dates should earn your trust. Take sensible precautions to protect yourself against those who don't have your best interests at heart. Do your research, as much as possible, and let trusted friends know when you are going back to a guy's place.

2. If an untidy house bothers you, be aware that even if you like the guy, his messiness will be an issue when you are co-habiting. When a house moves beyond mess into squalor, there may be more serious issues to be addressed.

3. Some people have been terribly hurt by their ex, but remember you are their date, not their counsellor.

Chapter 9

James

Erectile dysfunction is such a harsh term. Why not just call it Sleepy Peepee?

- Unknown

James was an English tourist, visiting members of his extended family who had relocated from the UK to Australia. He was young, single and looking for a good time.

He and Tinderella had chatted for a while online and moved onto texting each other directly on their personal phone numbers. This wasn't something Tinderella normally did, but since James wasn't a local, it was easier to do it this way. He was a friendly lad, as English as English gets. Very polite, well dressed and could hold an interesting conversation.

They decided to meet up.

Tinderella would play tour guide and although there was no promise of any intimacy, she thought a nice evening out with an English tourist might prove to be fun! She picked him up from his uncle's house, where he was staying. The plan was to go into the city for dinner. It was a beautiful summer night, with clear starry skies and a light breeze, the perfect backdrop for a good time.

Tinderella arrived at James's address and messaged him she was parked in the driveway. She had dressed for dinner, wearing her new, red skinny jeans and a low-necked black chiffon top, with her favourite shiny black stilettos. Her waterhole bracelet, made into a necklace by black ribbon added to each end to extend the length, completed the outfit. She'd styled her hair into a low bun. She felt very sexy!

James came into view within a few minutes. He was pleasant looking and had a wonderful big smile on his face. This was the icebreaker Tinderella had hoped for. His smile created an atmosphere of calm and it was exactly what the moment needed. She was still very nervous when it came to the dating game. It really takes a lot of courage to go out and meet people you don't know, to introduce yourself to a guy who may or may not offer any prospects beyond the first date. But Tinderella knew the alternative was not an option.

Dating is a game for the brave.

James was now real; he was sitting beside her and began to make idle chitchat. What is it about a guy and an accent? Tinderella found it so sexy. She hadn't dated many men with accents, so this was a new experience for her. She had to listen hard to understand what James was saying so she could respond in the right way, with the correct reply.

He told Tinderella of his business back in London and his life there. He was a regular visitor, travelling over to Australia every year. The minutes passed by quickly and they arrived at the Italian restaurant. It had great food and was one of Tinderella's favourite places to eat. James suggested they go for a drink first. It was obvious he was very keen on Tinderella when he strategically arranged the bar stools so their legs interlocked as they sat down.

James ordered their drinks then locked eyes with Tinderella.

'You are very beautiful,' he said.

Tinderella blushed and ducked her head. Compliments made her feel insecure, shy almost. It had been so long since someone complimented her on her looks. She was way out of her comfort zone. Wouldn't it be nice, she wondered, if more guys felt comfortable to compliment their partners sincerely just as James had done? A sincere compliment really is one of life's blessings and a beautiful gift to give to someone. It doesn't cost anything, only time and a warm smile, to make others feel valued.

Before long, James leant in to kiss her lips; they were ready, slightly open and moist from the lip-gloss Tinderella had applied earlier. His lips were warm and tender, not too wet, and his tongue played with her mouth in a delicate but playful way. He was a great kisser, and he knew it. Tinderella enjoyed the moment. It was sending shivers up her back and a sudden warm glow came over her body.

Leaning back, he said, 'I've been wanting to do that to you since I saw you.'

Tinderella giggled and smiled with her eyes, reaching for her drink. Oh my goodness, she thought, I need to empty this glass to get my confidence happening. Her heart was pounding in a nervous panic.

What if he wants more?

How will I do this?

We still have dinner to get through!

As if reading the thought bubbles exploding above Tinderella's head, James smiled, a reassuring smile, a peaceful one. It instantly relaxed Tinderella and made her feel more comfortable. They soon finished their drinks, and it was time for their meal. Conversation over dinner was a mixture of laughter, giggles and little jokes by James. He was very good at putting ladies at ease, which made him even more appealing. The meal was just enough, and very tasty with all fresh ingredients.

James suggested they go to another bar close by so they could sit and continue to talk some more. Tinderella was happy with this suggestion, and she held his hand as they walked along, chatting happily. She had consumed a couple of glasses of wine with dinner and knew she would need to leave her car in the city overnight. She wished she'd ordered an Uber in the first instance, to save the cost of overnight parking.

The bar was buzzing, and it was challenging to find a quiet place to sit so they could hear each other talk. They found a small table in the back of the bar with just one stool. James made it his mission to find a second stool; it wasn't long before he returned. He had a stool, but it was very different to Tinderella's, at least a foot or two lower. When James sat on it, he looked like the floor was swallowing him up. It made Tinderella laugh.

The night had been fun and relaxed—it was refreshing to meet a guy who wasn't too full-on.

The conversation kept flowing and so did the drinks. Tinderella was feeling quite tipsy and had a suspicion this was part of James's plan. And yes, she challenged him on it.

'What, me?' he replied, denying her playful accusation with a look of total shock and horror on his face. He then invited her to dance. The dance floor was small, but it would still work. It was only two-thirds full, and they left their jackets to secure their seats for their return.

James was a very good dancer, and he soon took the lead in every genre of music they danced to. He guided her through every move and held her securely, knowing her legs were a bit wobbly at times.

Half a dozen songs later, they returned to their seats and James leant into Tinderella and kissed her passionately on the lips. She accepted it gratefully. He pulled her from her stool and held her tightly in his arms. Tinderella melted. It was so out of character for her, but it had been so long since a kind man had held her, and felt such a warm connection, albeit a small one.

She needed to keep her head.

James was a tourist, and he wasn't invested in anything long-term. Tinderella understood this was never going to be forever. It was just a fleeting romance. Was she emotionally ready to deal with unbelievable sex and a night of bodies entwining in lust and sweat?

Tinderella was indeed ready.

The signal was given in a look she sent James, and he asked her to go back to his place. She agreed. After finding a taxi, they soon arrived at his uncle's place. Fortunately, he had privacy in a room located at the end of the house. They were soon pulling at each other's clothes, and James made a joke about Britain and Australia being united.

Their lips locked, their bodies intertwined, and they were kissing passionately on the bed. Tinderella felt sexually aroused, and in the moment—held close in his arms, she was ready to make love to him.

And then, with their emotions charged and pulses racing, the atmosphere changed. James lost his erection.

What was a girl to say? What was a girl to do?

He was very upset and talked to his penis with disgust. He told it that it had let the team and his country down, calling it every name known to man, swearing at it whilst making rapid arm movements. He was so apologetic to Tinderella, telling her this was something that happened in the movies, not to him, and not in real life. He was clearly pissed off and disappointed.

Tinderella tried her very best to bring his member to attention, but it wasn't possible. The night was over. Well, at least the sex part. What a disappointment. She wasn't quite sure what to do next. James was still trying to work out why it had happened and told her it was because his uncle was home, and it was playing on his mind. It had totally unfocused and distracted him. She tried her best to reassure him and tell him it was okay... although, actually it wasn't. Tinderella had invested some serious time into this night, including payment for drinks and parking and now she was up for two more Uber fares.

There was nothing she could do to change it. It was over, and the easiest thing was to make a quick getaway.

She ordered her Uber and James sat with her as they waited, a look of pure disappointment on his face. With the Uber's arrival time confirmed, he walked her to the door and waited with her outside at the pick-up point. He was so disappointed, and so polite. He apologised yet again, and it allowed Tinderella to smile reassuringly at him as she climbed into the back seat of the Uber.

It took her away into the night, and just like that, she was swept away from James and his limp member. Tinderella was never to hear from him again.

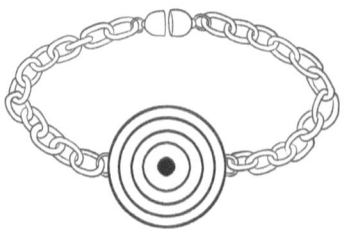

It's Time to Talk… by Simone

PRACTISE DATE SAFETY BASICS

Keep your phone number to yourself

Tinderella has a sound policy in not giving out your phone number to potential dates. It's best to keep messages within the online dating app until after you have met your guy—preferably more than once. Only hand out your phone number if you feel comfortable with him. You never know if someone will end up being a stalker. You can always block their number, but prevention is better than cure in this case.

Keep an eye on how much you drink when you're on a date

I think we can all relate to having a drink or two to bolster our confidence before a date, as Tinderella did. Just make sure you know your own limits, and keep track of your alcoholic drinks, (including the ones you have consumed before you leave home!). Alcohol impairs our executive brain function, so when you're tipsy it's harder to think clearly. Not to mention the effects of the 'beer goggles'. It's amazing how awesome a guy can seem as the night wears on and you're having a few drinks. You certainly don't want to regret your actions the next day because of how much you drank the night before! And if you're planning to drive to meet your date and drive home safely afterwards, you'll need to make sure you're under the legal blood alcohol limit.

National guidelines for alcohol consumption state that drinking no more than four standard drinks on a single occasion reduces the risk of alcohol-related injury arising from that one occasion[8]. Those same guidelines recommend women drink no more than one standard drink per hour to stay under the legal limit of 0.05%. Other factors to consider when counting your drinks to stay within the legal limit are

---

[8] http://www.alcohol.gov.au/internet/alcohol/publishing.nsf/Content/guide-adult

your metabolism and your size. Smaller women and women with more body fat will feel the effects of alcohol quicker than taller, thinner women. If you're drinking on an empty stomach, the alcohol will hit you harder and faster. It's also a good idea to avoid mixing your drinks as this can speed up the effects of alcohol and cause some people to fill ill during the night (and make the hangover much worse the next day).

To reduce the effects of alcohol, try pacing yourself by having a glass of still or sparkling water between each alcoholic drink. Or take your own bottle of water with you to sip during the evening and remember to eat something as you go.

ACCENTS AND ATTRACTION

It's interesting that both men and women tend to love foreign accents. According to a recent poll, the New Zealand accent is rated as the sexiest in the world, closely followed by the South African accent[9]. The Irish accent is in third place and in fifth place is the wonderful Aussie accent!

Psychology plays a big part in our love of accents. When we hear a person speaking with an accent, it can create an unconscious yearning for travel, adventure and new experiences, making their speech incredibly captivating to the listener's ears. We also tend to associate a country with a particularly desirable aspect of culture. For example, we associate France—and so French accents—with romance; British accents and intelligence; South American accents and all things exotic. It's just another wonderful element that can play a part in attraction between two people.

---

[9] https://bigseventravel.com/2019/04/worlds-sexiest-accent/

How to accept a compliment

From a psychological perspective, praise and reward increases a person's sense of self-worth and confidence, and the person receiving the compliment will find the praise-giver more endearing for their kind words. Our level of comfort in receiving a compliment is an indicator of how we value ourselves.

People with low self-esteem will feel very uncomfortable receiving compliments. They will tend to brush them off, because the compliment contradicts how they feel about themselves. This reaction can actually be quite hurtful to the person giving the compliment. A compliment is a gift and should not be refused or devalued. When someone compliments you, if you feel compelled to deflect or dismiss what they are saying about you (or your outfit, or the meal you've made or anything else) try saying a simple 'thank you'. Lean slightly forward, look the giver in the eyes, and give them a sincere smile as you say it.

Feeling that a compliment is not warranted or genuine?

Sometimes people try to flatter another person because they want something in return. Their compliments are not genuine and are given with the intent they'll get something back in return. This could range from seeking a return compliment or praise from you to satisfy their own ego or lack of self-esteem, to wanting you to comply/oblige to having sex. Compliments are sincere. Flattery is self-serving.

Dealing with disappointment in the bedroom

Tinderella had a fun night with her date. Drinks, laughs and dancing made for a memorable evening. For those who look forward to even more fun in the bedroom at the end of the night, if the guy has an erection problem, the evening can become memorable for all the wrong reasons. Tinderella's warm and sociable personality means

James would have felt confident in her company, so his inability to perform in bed at the end of the date was a shame for them both.

Why do men have erection problems?

Not being able to 'get it up' and keep it up in the moment is fairly common. Perhaps you can relate to Tinderella's experience with James? Knowing this was likely to be a one-night-only experience probably put a lot of pressure on him, which impacted his ability to relax and enjoy the moment they had been building toward all evening. Whether it's a one-off or an ongoing experience, it can be extraordinarily embarrassing for a guy—especially during his first performance with a woman.

Having trouble getting or keeping an erection can happen from time to time. It can be due to factors like anxiety and stress or having drunk too much alcohol. Some men also claim that wearing a condom can affect their ability to raise and keep a consistent erection, but this should never be a 'get out of jail free card' for a guy to avoid wearing one. You can help him maintain his erection and to 'recover' for another round by gently stroking his balls or other erotic foreplay. Google is a friend here, with plenty of ideas to light your man's fire just a mouse click away.

If this is an ongoing problem, there is a chance it is being caused by a physical condition such as heart disease or diabetes. We don't know if this was the case for James. His explanation was he was distracted by his uncle being at home. He felt very deflated (pun intended) by his lack of performance, which would have made the situation worse. In case you were wondering, calling his penis names wouldn't have made any difference at all to the situation, other than as an attempt at humour or self-flagellation to reduce his embarrassment.

Having an erection fail is a blow to a man's pride, and his ego (his identity i.e. how he sees himself or who he believes he is). He may think when it happens, the show is over. He may also be so embarrassed and annoyed at himself he no longer wants to have sex. He may blame himself as James did, and will express his frustration at himself as if he is the sole initiator and conductor of the sexual act—taking on all responsibility for both of you to achieve orgasm.

The best response that *both* of you can make in this situation is to keep going with the sex! You're still attracted to each other, so don't break the intimacy between you.

You are not the cause of the problem

Sometimes, when a man loses his erection or can't achieve one, a woman can feel she must be the problem. She may think the guy doesn't find her attractive enough to have sex with. This is rarely the case.

There are things the woman can do to help a guy have an erection, including taking the focus off his penis and enjoying foreplay on other areas of the guy's body. Find out what he likes and go with it. Explore his body with your fingers, your tongue. Give him a head job, but if the oral sex isn't helping, that's okay too. Try something else. You could turn the focus back to you and ask him to pleasure you; you could masturbate in front of him; or use his fingers to do it for you. Bringing you to orgasm will give him a sense of achievement, which will also help reduce embarrassment on his part, whether he can have an erection and intercourse with you.

LEARNINGS FROM TINDERELLA AND JAMES:

1. Be safe. Don't give out your phone number to a guy until you're very comfortable with him. Count your alcohol drinks during any outing with your date. It's best to remain within healthy and legal alcohol limits, particularly if you're driving, and to avoid the 'beer goggles' effect.

2. Give and receive compliments—they are a gift.

3. An erection fail can happen for many reasons. When it happens, there is no need for intimacy and sexual pleasure to also stop in that moment. There are many ways to arouse and pleasure a guy besides direct penis stimulation, as there are for women, so a

failed erection shouldn't prevent you from having an orgasm or two.

Chapter 10

Nigel

We should be happy some things didn't work out as we wanted or expected. Oftentimes, we dodge bullets we didn't even see coming.

- Lloyd Barker

After James and his unpatriotic penis, Tinderella decided to take things just a little slower. She would get to know the guy before the physical side of things took over and created a total distraction from the other parts of the relationship. Tinderella still believed in finding the 'right' relationship. To her mind, this took three main elements; mental, physical and spiritual.

These three key elements represented what she thought of as the relationship triangle. A perfect balance of the three would give Tinderella a holistic life partner, a potential soul mate who would provide her with the support she needed in all aspects of life. This was her relationship goal.

If the elements were unbalanced, she believed the relationship would fall apart. Baz had proven to her that although the physical side of their connection was exciting and their time together had been lovely and lustful, the other elements were not present. And she craved mental stimulation, conversations that tested her beliefs, and the spiritual interests that intrigued her. Sadly, Baz hadn't been able to hold her interest in that way. Surely she couldn't spend twenty-four hours a day in bed with him. Could she? Let's just leave that question unanswered.

She would need to practice patience, something which Tinderella had very little of. She would need to spend more time with her dates to find out about their common interests, to see if they had compatible triangles, and in the end, to know whether they were truly meant to be together.

Tinderella had stayed on two of the main dating sites, even though she hadn't been an 'active' member, and she had received messages from several men.

This was how she met Nigel.

Nigel made her heart sing. He seemed like one of the kindest human beings God had ever created. Tinderella wasn't looking at the physical this time; she was looking at the person as a complete individual. She wasn't superficial or egotistical, and she had a tender heart that overflowed with empathy and compassion. This trait, she vowed, she would never change for anyone.

Nigel had the same level of compassion and care. He had a childlike gentleness about him that made him seem vulnerable. Tinderella could feel the need to nurture him, protect him. He seemed extraordinarily open as they connected online, sharing the good and bad of his life. He had been single for a long period of time because of the way he had suffered in relationships in the past. He told Tinderella he had been a target for women who had used and abused him, emotionally and financially. He had become a human punching bag for their wants and desires, leaving him feeling fractured, timid and reserved.

He admitted his childhood had left him vulnerable to this treatment, as his father and uncle had, as part of a paedophilia ring, molested him between the age of six and thirteen. He had also watched his mother be beaten and sexually abused during the course of her long relationship with his father. She had committed suicide after a night of sexual trauma left her hospitalised. It was the only way she knew to escape the volatile relationship. Nigel was eleven years old, and the weight started to pile on.

He had become bedridden at times, unable to physically stand under his own body mass. His doctors had warned him he was a walking heart attack, living on borrowed time. When his partners found his physical body repulsive, and personal hygiene had become a challenge for him, he knew things had to change. As a result, eight years prior, he had had surgery to reduce his stomach size. He had shed almost one hundred kilograms off his exhausted body. His organs and limbs, which had suffered under the constant pressure of his once-obese body, were weak and needed further medical attention if he were to see another twenty years of life. He was only forty-four years old.

Tinderella had not seen Nigel without his clothes, as it was early days. He had been sharing his journey with her via online messenger and took pains to be open about his recovery process and how his body appeared now. He had retained excess skin on his body, which weighed close to 30 kilograms and hung from his frame like empty bags, his stomach skin draping almost to his knees. He was unable to make progress at the moment, as he couldn't afford the much-needed skin surgery to complete his new body. To have the skin taken off and his body reconstructed, not only did he need the money to have the procedure, he also needed his organs to be strong enough to recover from the 18-hour surgery.

She tried to be understanding, as she could see from pictures the pressure, commitment and time it had taken Nigel to lose the ninety-five kilograms from his 6'3" frame. His height was deceiving because he often stood with a slight hunch, a consequence of carrying so much excess weight over the years. Other than his height, Nigel was an ordinary-looking man. To borrow from the Australian TV series Kath and Kim, he could be likened to a milk arrowroot biscuit—plain and unexciting. He wasn't comfortable in social environments. In his mind, Nigel was still obese and had many issues to deal with from his past.

He was fragile and Tinderella understood why. She had never heard of anyone going through such a rollercoaster of trauma. Nigel had blamed himself for it all when he was younger, even though his experiences had caused him insurmountable emotional, mental and physical pain. These early chats with him made Tinderella reluctant to keep on conversing with him. The last thing she wanted to do was to become part of Nigel's bigger problem. How would he handle rejection if it didn't work out in his favour? Surely he was emotionally fragile after his past life experiences?

Nigel assured her that he was ready to meet new people, and that doing so would help him overcome his reservations and conquer the fear-based beliefs from his past. It would help him feel empowered and set him on a new life path that would give him a life purpose, something he had never had before. He had been married three times, although children had never resulted from those unions. He revealed to Tinderella he was an emotional partner, not a sexual one, and that he lacked the ability to sustain an erection, let alone orgasm. This was possibly the reason why his relationships didn't last.

Tinderella, as we know, was empathetic. These revelations made her ponder whether it was worth investing time in this connection with Nigel. Why was a man like this, with such a perfect soul, alone and looking for love in the online universe?

As they messaged, Tinderella had learnt he was intelligent and enjoyed studying. Nigel had a degree in communication management, which she found impressive. More than that, he was an expert at understanding people, and he would dissect their perspectives in a clear and analytical way.

Everything that came up in conversation with him would be turned into a great debate in which Nigel would quickly elevate himself as the subject matter expert. Tinderella was impressed with his knowledge of people and business. He seemed unreal, almost too good for her. She felt lucky she had finally found someone who could keep her interest intellectually. It was an important part of the triangle she needed in her future partner. She wasn't sure about the sexual attraction as yet. Knowing of his past and the trauma he had to deal with as a young child and carried into adulthood, Tinderella wasn't certain he was capable of the kind of relationship she needed. Was it pity she felt for him, or guilt at her own easier life that finally made her decide to meet with him?

I'm sure I'll know when I meet him, she thought. She would keep her wits about her and be logical about her future decisions where this man was concerned.

Nigel wasn't a social drinker and wasn't one to go out to bars or clubs, so Tinderella suggested a quiet modern café where they could hear each other talk, and see if there was a physical and mental attraction.

The time was set for lunch the following day. It was an early date by Tinderella's standard, and she would have to rework her workday schedule to arrive at the agreed time.

In her mind, she had already chosen what she would wear. A navy blue dress with slits in the arms, a slit in the side of the skirt, and low-cut cleavage was her choice. It was stylish and comfortable. She was pleased—she was becoming an expert at choosing just the right date outfit, in her mind. Her beloved waterhole bracelet would stay on her wrist. It had become such a part of her, and it complemented so many of the different styles and colours she selected for each of her much-anticipated dates.

The café they had chosen to meet at was quiet, with just a handful of customers in the shop. This made it easy to find a table out of the way of others. As Tinderella settled into her seat, a large bulky man approached her, smiling. It was Nigel. His face showed he was happy with the woman sitting before him. Tinderella herself was not yet certain of the man opposite her. He was physically unattractive, but he had a kindness she could see in his eyes.

As they sat and chatted, she began to process this man before her. He showed a genuine interest in her, asking a constant flow of questions about what she liked to do, and they soon found they had a lot in common.

Tinderella was impressed Nigel had very similar spiritual views to her and was open to all the universe offered. She found herself laughing and enjoying his company. He was witty, intelligent and had a wicked sense of humour. He had lived through some amazing life experiences and achieved so much on a personal level. He was driven in his business career, with several major ambitions. One was to become a leader in his local community, and he was already achieving that through sitting on several well-known boards in the charity and non-profit space. He was already gaining traction with local politicians, and he had met and become friends with many business leaders.

Tinderella hadn't realised how quickly time had passed and her body was telling her it was time to eat. She asked Nigel if he was a little bit peckish and he agreed that they should have something to eat. However, he had forgotten to bring his card wallet in with him, and he had already used his cash to buy the coffee that was now sitting empty on the table.

This didn't perturb Tinderella, and she brushed his comment aside, saying it was her turn to pay. Nigel smiled at her and told her how generous her gesture was. The food soon came to the table and their conversation flowed, mostly about Tinderella and her past marriage, her dating experiences and her family life. Nigel asked after her successful business and he seemed impressed in turn when she spoke of her successful investments in properties, locally and interstate.

Suddenly Nigel began to look awkward, almost uncomfortable. The shift in him was clear, and Tinderella was confused and a little taken aback by the sudden change in his behaviour. He continued to shift uncomfortably in his seat, showing signs of agitation. At this point he looked at his phone then apologised to Tinderella, saying he had a meeting to attend, and although he would rather stay and chat to her, he couldn't postpone it. He apologised and stood to leave, all the while watching Tinderella and her reaction. There was an awkward silence.

'Please, let's have another coffee soon?'

Tinderella nodded in silence and watched him exit through the glass sliding door and disappear amongst the pedestrians crowding the walkway outside.

She could sense a person very close to her, so she refocused her attention onto the woman standing by her table. The lady asked to sit with Tinderella, then pulled a chair out from the table to sit directly opposite her.

'Hello,' she said. 'You don't know me. My name is Pauline, and I want to tell you something about the man you were just with. Please allow me time to talk—I'm not sure how long you've been seeing him, but I need you to hear what I have to say.'

Tinderella sat and listened to Pauline unfold the story of her past relationship with Nigel. It was short, only five months, but it was long enough for her to witness the real Nigel and uncover the truth behind his 'stories'.

It quickly became clear to Tinderella that most things Nigel had told her were untrue.

Pauline confirmed that Nigel was a pathological liar and suffered from narcissistic personality disorder. He was a con artist. He had the ability to attract empathic women and focused on single mums who were established and financially viable.

Tinderella was speechless. Her intuition had tried to warn her, but she had mistaken it for guilt. She had a very important lesson in front of her. Tinderella sat, motionless, whilst the woman in front of her began to explain.

'Dr. Google defines a person with narcissist personality disorder as having an inflated sense of self-importance and are often pathological liars. Narcissists are very good at presenting themselves as victims, lonely and compassionate. Almost child-like, and maybe this is what attracts an empathic woman to date a narcissist. Every decision and action are always about his or her own personal agenda. There is only one person within the narcissistic relationship—the narcissist.

Tinderella listened, her mouth starting to go dry, and she found the questions she wanted to ask stuck in her throat. All she could do was stare at Pauline who sat opposite her.

'As their partner, you are ideally there to provide fuel for them. Remember, such a person doesn't have the ability to love, to be compassionate or to empathise. Everything the narcissist may say, message or do is completely rehearsed and has been practiced on many past victims of their fractured relationships,' Pauline continued.

Tinderella managed to speak up. 'Please. You're saying Nigel is this terrible thing... a narcissist. I need to hear evidence. I need to understand your pain.'

'All right. Nigel will tell you he is highly intelligent, but the truth is, he barely got through high school. He'll tell you he is highly educated and holds a degree in communications, which he doesn't. He was never a communications expert in the Australian Federal Police. He isn't childless—he has seven children from four different women. He was not brought up in traumatic family circumstances. He actually had an uneventful childhood, and he wanted for nothing. He was well cared for and grew up in a nurturing environment. His parents still live in a small coastal town, up north.'

Tinderella tried to process the information she was hearing. She couldn't understand how someone could feel the need to lie so dramatically about their past, their present and their future. The clock on the wall now read 3:30pm, but Tinderella needed to know more.

'Look,' Pauline said, 'my best advice to you is to watch the Netflix series Dirty John, which is based on the relationship between Debra Newell and John Meehan. John was a sociopath with narcissistic personality disorder. If you are going to pursue anything further with Nigel, at least be informed and educated.'

The woman reached for Tinderella's hand and patted it. 'I'm here for you, sweetheart, if you need anything. This man deceived me, and I hope that you pay some mind to my words of warning. Here is my number,' she said, as she pulled out a card from her purse. With that, Pauline got up, said goodbye, and she too disappeared into the kaleidoscope of shoppers in the street.

Tinderella sank into her chair, staring at the café's doors as she thought about everything Pauline had said. In such a short amount of time, she had been given so much information to think about. This was supposed to be a simple coffee date, but Tinderella knew it had turned into so much more. Thanks to Pauline, it was the biggest learning curve of her dating life.

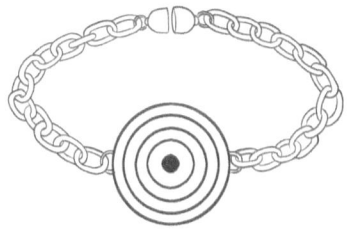

It's Time to Talk... by Simone

DEFINE YOUR 'RIGHT' RELATIONSHIP

Tinderella believed the right relationship for her needed to have a balance of the mental, physical and spiritual. These categories guide her in choosing the important traits and qualities of the man she is looking for in her online dating journey. It's great to see her list is being honed and refined as she dates different guys. She is enjoying the learnings along her dating journey and as a result, is becoming clearer about what she is looking for in a life partner.

When we're not clear about what we want in a guy, or in a relationship, then it's easier to settle for someone who makes us feel good in some ways—but not in others. Chapter 2 provides suggestions for writing your wish list of the traits you are looking for in your future partner (*K.I.S.S. List for Mr Right*), and Chapter 4 provides guidance for writing your wish list of the traits of the relationship you want to have with a future partner. More guidance is also available on our website: www.tinderella.com/resources

Once you have written your 'wish lists', it's important to stick to it as much as possible. Work out in advance which of the items on your list are a must have. These are your 'deal-breakers'. If a guy doesn't tick one or more of these boxes, he isn't the right guy for you. Also take the time to identify the items on your list that are moderately important, and those that are more of a 'nice-to-have'.

While we're all only human and it may seem a bit rich to set such a high bar for your future partner, you shouldn't talk yourself into accepting him if he doesn't meet your deal-breakers. Don't try to convince yourself you can change or 'fix' him to make him fit the list. You will only make both of you miserable if you try. And once you do meet someone who satisfies the things that matter most to you, then accept that lovely person for who he is, even if the nice-to-haves aren't all there.

TAME THE EMOTIONAL ROLLERCOASTER OF ONLINE DATING

The dating journey is a tricky one because you are not just guided by your head, you're also influenced by your heart. And you need both! Depending on how your past choices and experiences have turned out, it can be easy to ignore one over the other.

When emotions are at play, it can be challenging to apply logic or reasoning to your decisions and actions as the wiring in your brain doesn't easily allow for emotions and logic to co-exist in the same moment. Neuroscience indicates emotions primarily drive the choices we make, while practicality and objectivity (logic) have a lesser role in decision-making. You only need to look at the psychology of marketing to see people buy on emotion and justify on logic. This is why women sometimes make too many allowances for a guy, ignoring not only their wish list but also their intuition.

Create your wish lists before you embark on your dating journey, while your emotions aren't in play—knowing, of course, that you can update it along the way.

BEWARE THE NARCISSIST

It is difficult to pick a narcissist on the first date, or even after a few dates, as they are master manipulators. Being in a relationship with a guy who is a narcissist can be extraordinarily damaging to a woman; to her confidence; her sense of self-worth; her body image; her friendship circles; relationships with her family; her mental and/or physical health, and more.

Narcissists are often difficult to identify because these people initially come across as confident, charming and intelligent. They are also usually drawn to gentle, sensitive partners who are both giving and forgiving. Once a narcissist has a woman under his spell the manipulation takes an even stronger hold, until the woman feels almost broken.

Narcissists don't handle criticism well, and they don't like being challenged on their beliefs. They can easily adopt the role of the martyr in these situations, causing the woman to doubt herself or question her own intentions around raising her concerns. Narcissists play on people's doubts and fears because they don't want their true selves (or their web of lies) to be revealed. They also don't like it when people have a different opinion to their own.

Narcissism traits checklist:
- Compulsive liar
- Lack of empathy
- Highly critical—of their partner, their partner's friends, family, career, hobbies, etc. Sometimes their criticism is disguised as a back-handed compliment.
- Exaggerated sense of self-importance (they may lie about their achievements)
- Hypersensitive to criticism
- Exploits or manipulates others for personal gain (although they deny this if confronted)
- Arrogance
- Sense of entitlement
- Exerts control over their partner through emotional manipulation. Their actions and words will either 'push' their partner away (e.g. silent treatment, criticisms) or 'pull' their partner towards them (e.g. love-bombing, gifts).
- Low self-esteem (dislike of self, constantly needs praise)
- Likes to talk about themselves—a lot
- Brings others down with backstabbing and jealousy

It is very difficult for narcissists to have deep, fulfilling relationships as they have to learn, or at least learn to imitate, the emotions of empathy and emotional intelligence—traits they don't possess. They often leave a trail of broken women behind them. Narcissists fall under the same category of personality disorders that includes sociopaths and psychopaths[10]. Narcissistic Personality Disorder is a diagnosable mental health condition, but due to the nature of narcissism, sufferers are unlikely to seek help[11].

DEALING WITH A NARCISSIST

Intelligence is not enough. Seek social support. It is not surprising Pauline was keen to intervene to prevent Tinderella from experiencing the pain and deception of being in a relationship with Nigel. Many victims feel compelled to warn others away once they've escaped the clutches of a narcissist.

Those fortunate enough to have freed themselves from such a relationship express surprise that they didn't see through their narcissistic ex-partner's behaviours. Looking back, they may recognise the impact their ex-partner was having on their confidence and self-worth, but at the time, they possibly felt they were under his spell, defying all logic as to why it took them so long to leave.

One reason women stay in narcissistic relationships is because they have been gaslighted by their narcissist partners for some time, and so they ignore their own instincts about what is really going on in their relationship. As mentioned, narcissists are usually compulsive liars—and they are exceptionally good at it.

Typically, the narcissist's constant negative, niggling comments will wear down a woman's self-esteem, which is why even the most confident, intelligent woman can end up feeling like a shell of who she once was. She is likely to need to rebuild herself from the inside out after leaving a narcissistic relationship, and it can take a long time (sometimes years) for her to truly heal and learn to trust herself and others again.

Even the keenest intelligence is no match for a narcissist, due to the physiological changes that occur in a woman while she's in a rela-

---

[10] https://www.betterhelp.com/advice/sociopathy/dsm-5-sociopath-diagnostic-definitions-and-symptoms/

[11] http://dsm.wikia.com/wiki/Narcissistic_Personality_Disorder

tionship with such a person. Just as we can become physically and psychologically addicted to a substance (drugs, alcohol, sugar) or an experience (gambling, shopping, sex, work), we can also become addicted to love, or to a person—particularly when we are in the hands of a narcissist[12].

A narcissist uses emotional manipulation to light up the same pain and pleasure receptors in the brain that see us fall into other forms of addiction. The woman feels the same 'rush', the same highs and cravings (particularly during any attempts to quit her addiction—the relationship) and the same inevitable downers as any addict. The first step in quitting or overcoming any addiction is to recognise there is indeed an addiction. It's at this low point that a woman will need to rely on willpower to abstain, as well as the critical support of friends and family, to leave her narcissistic partners.

Unfortunately for many, a woman's loss of self-esteem and confidence, coupled with the pressure of addiction, will often cause her to return. If children are involved, it makes it even more difficult for the woman to break free. This is a similar cycle to victims of domestic violence and may need similar levels of strong support to resolve.

If you have missed the signs of narcissism in the early stages of dating and are now in a relationship with a guy who you suspect may be a narcissist, remember you always have choices. Trust your intuition and know that you don't have to stay in a situation—relationship, job or community—if it is no longer serving you. Life is short. Don't settle for less than you deserve. If your self-esteem has taking a battering, then look deeper inside yourself to find that part of you that knows this to be true.

Your closest friends and family are the best source of support here. Ask them to remind you of your special qualities and to support you as you find a way forward that feels right for you. No matter what your narcissistic partner may tell you, drawing on their support is not selfish—it's part of a healthy community, and provides your friends

---

[12] https://theanatomyoflove.com/conclusions/first-study-romance-reward-system/

and family with the opportunity to show you how much they care about you.

LEARNINGS FROM TINDERELLA AND NIGEL:

1. Be clear about what matters most to you, and the type of person you want to ultimately spend the rest of your life with. It's okay to be super fussy! Stick to your checklist of the values and character traits you do and don't want in a guy. Remember to give the relationship a few months to develop before letting yourself become emotionally embroiled with a guy. Narcissistic traits, like other less positive traits, take time to reveal themselves. When they do, trust your instincts... and run!

2. While online dating is prevalent in our modern age, meeting and dating men this way rather than through traditional avenues provides no greater guarantee of success. You may still meet a narcissist, a player, or men with other worrying traits. It is essential you take responsibility for your own physical and emotional safety and take the time to listen to your intuition.

3. If you are hurting—for any reason—reach out for support. If you are finding it difficult to shake feelings of despair, thoughts of self-harm or symptoms of depression or anxiety, please see your doctor. There is help out there and you will get through this.

Chapter 11

Joe

'Meow' means 'woof' in cat.
- George Carlin

Joe was a real charmer. He was quick-witted and cheeky, and Tinderella really enjoyed his online company. Soon they had agreed to meet for coffee. She chose a coffee shop in her local area as she liked to be able to leave quickly if she needed to make a getaway.

Tinderella arrived early, hoping to find a pleasant seat that offered a little privacy from other patrons. She'd chosen to wear her flowing lime-green maxi dress that tied around her waist and accentuated her ample bosom. She felt very feminine and free. The colour worked beautifully with her hazel eyes and made them look even greener. She wore her good luck charm, of course. She had tied thin black leather straps to the ends of her prized silver waterhole bracelet and secured it provocatively around her neck.

She sat watching the door and waiting to see Joe's smiling face. He arrived, followed by a powerful positive energy. A true free spirit, he was well known for practicing energy healings and followed several modalities such as reiki. He was also gifted in the skill of rebirthing for those who had trauma and loss in their past. Joe had the ability to heal people and bring them back to their full potential.

He was well known in spiritual circles and often spoke about his gift and ways people could become happier in themselves by living at a higher vibrational level. This was a type of healing that helped complete the mind, body and spirit triangle. During their online exchanges, Joe often said he was baffled the spirit side was so undervalued and left virtually unattended. Helping and healing people with lopsided triangles was an important part of his life. Balance was his mantra.

Joe's lips were warm and tender as he greeted Tinderella with a kiss on the cheek. He ordered a green tea with jasmine. Tinderella had already placed her order and much to Joe's disgust, the waitress delivered a double skinny mocha to her.

'Why you drink that rubbish is beyond me,' Joe said with a laugh. Tinderella knew he was just having a little fun with her, but she felt a slight tinge of guilt in looking at her coffee. Not enough to stop her drinking it, and it tasted amazing!

Joe sat next to her, and she looked deep into his crystal clear, emerald green eyes as they talked and talked. His eyes were hypnotic, and it was easy to get lost in their pure colour. Tinderella felt as though they could see deep into her soul. As their eyes connected, her heart fluttered and skipped a beat.

It was a beautiful evening. The sunset glowed warmly, slowly dimming as night fell. Tinderella didn't want her time with Joe to end, he was addictive and shared some amazing stories from his global escapades. Fighting with the darkness, she quietly suggested they go to her house and have a drink there before he had to go back to his hotel. He was only in town for one night but Tinderella had spent a lot of time in conversation with Joe online, and then through the recent few phone calls, she felt she had been able to get to know him pretty well.

Joe agreed, and they were soon sitting in her home. It was a four-bedroom house, with plenty of space for herself and her two children. The house had open living areas and an outdoor alfresco area towards the back of the property and Tinderella had converted the fourth bedroom into her office. It was modern in style and furnished with warmth and love. Many items were secondhand or had been sourced online at a great price. Tinderella had developed the knack of recycling, buying used and collectable furniture and turning it over. She liked to say it was the perfect way to achieve a champagne lifestyle on a beer budget. Tinderella was comfortable in her home, and it showed, as she became very relaxed sitting with Joe on the couch.

The conversation flowed, and they chatted easily together. Joe leant in to kiss her on the lips. She caught her breath for a moment. This was her dream man, and he was making a move to kiss her! Pinch me now, Tinderella thought.

But as Joe leant closer, his nose began to twitch, and his eyes glazed over.

He pulled away and Tinderella could see his face was breaking out in little red blotches. He rubbed at his eyes, which had started to swell.

Tinderella was dumbstruck! What on earth was happening?

'Are you okay?'

Joe was finding it difficult to speak. His throat was closing up and get scratchy.

'Do you have a cat?' he finally coughed out.

'Oh yes,' Tinderella said. 'I have three. They're gorgeous, my babies. They come in and out as they please. They've been with me through everything.'

Disaster!

Joe jumped up from the couch.

Why didn't you tell me?' he said angrily. 'I'm highly allergic to cats! I need to get out of here!'

With that, Joe was gone in a flash. Tinderella was frozen like a deer in the headlights, the vacated seat next to her still warm.

'What the heck just happened?' she asked the empty room. I'm sure I told him, she thought. Oh well… there was no way Tinderella was choosing between him and her beloved cats. Goodbye, Joe.

Bugger!

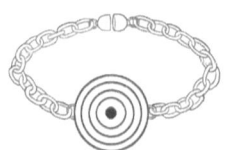

It's Time to Talk... by Simone

Meeting new people is a great way to expand your horizons and to learn more about life and the world through the experiences of others. The spiritual and psychic approach to learning and healing is a realm more and more people are interested in. If this isn't something that interests you, but your date has a passion for all things spiritual, then it may be an opportunity to ask questions and learn more about an area you hadn't previously explored.

A healthy relationship includes growth, and it allows room for both partners to pursue individual as well as mutual interests. So don't be too quick to write off that guy with an interest you don't share. Being open to the new is an essential element to bring to your dating journey.

PRACTISE DATE SAFETY BASICS

As you date, you may find yourself wanting to ask a man you hardly know back to your house for sex. Imagine the scenario—you're enjoying a fabulous evening out with a guy. You know there's a connection, maybe even some sexual chemistry brewing. You're feeling horny and you sense he is, too. You really, really want to have sex with this guy. You want to invite him back to your place, but you're unsure of how to broach this with him. Thoughts around rejection, personal safety and buyer's remorse may flash through your mind, but your body is screaming something very different. What to do?

Ultimately, it's your body and your choice. Here are some pointers to help you decide how to proceed with asking a guy home:
- Alcohol can impair your judgement, so if you've been drinking during the course of your date, make sure you listen to your intuition if it's been trying to warn you that all is not quite right with this guy. Having sex with him because you're horny is not worth the risk of enduring uncomfortable or un-

wanted, persistent contact from a guy who turns out to be a jerk.

- If what you're feeling is purely a physical attraction, rather than an emotional one, you could say: 'I've loved our evening. I'm not sure if I want a relationship with you, but right now I really want to just have sex with you. If you feel the same, would you like to come back to my place?'

- If you are emotionally drawn to him, as well as wanting to have sex with him, then you could say: 'I've loved our evening together. You have so many qualities I'm looking for in a guy, and I'd really love to see where things could progress between us. But right now, I just want to have sex with you. If you feel the same way, would you like to come back to my place?'

- Keep in mind that the guy may not mirror your emotional attraction to him, but you could end up having some fabulous sex. You may still progress to a beautiful relationship, or you may not see the guy again… Yet another scenario is that he could become your 'fuck buddy' or a friend-with-benefits while you continue on your dating journey.

- Personal safety is still of paramount importance when bringing a guy home for sex. Remember to use condoms—and ensure you have a supply on hand at home. You could also text a girlfriend beforehand to let her know what's happening. Include the guy's name and the details you do know.

DEALING WITH ALLERGIES

Pets can be a significant part of a person's life. As you get to know someone, this may be a factor one or both of you need to account for as you assess your compatibility. An allergic reaction to an animal type, though, is not fun, and must be addressed. The situation between Joe and Tinderella is quite a common one, where one person in a relationship is highly allergic and the other isn't.

Take responsibility for your allergies

When it comes to allergies, the number one rule is to take responsibility for your own needs. Allergies are invisible, so others around you are unlikely to be aware of the things that may or will trigger an uncomfortable or even a dangerous reaction in you. Whether it's you who has an allergy, or a potential date, it's up to the sufferer to avoid, as best as possible, the things they are allergic to. The sufferer can, as appropriate, inform others around them—such as meeting a new date for the first time—of how they can offer support. This is particularly important whenever a sufferer visits other people's homes.

Joe's reaction verged on blame. He was frustrated with Tinderella for not telling him she had cats. Her surprised and confused response indicates she didn't know of his allergies. She thought she had mentioned in passing she had cats, but the responsibility here lies with Joe, who has the allergy. Allergies can be life threatening, with some resulting in an anaphylactic reaction. Joe's immediate response to flee Tinderella's house may have been warranted for his own health, but his anger was unfair as he hadn't properly informed her beforehand of his needs.

Low allergy options

It can be distressing or frustrating when you want a cat or dog but can't have one because your partner is allergic. It can be even harder if it is your kids who want a pet, but you can't allow this because a parent or another family member is allergic. It is a reality for many families, though, and needs to be accepted for the wellbeing and safety of the person with allergies. Try to re-focus on positive alternatives such as a pet from a different category (e.g. a dog instead of a cat, or a bird instead of a dog), or look for a low-allergen option such as fish, hermit crabs, stick insects, lizards and so on.

For some couples, it may be possible to co-exist if one of them has an allergy to cats. A person with an allergy has an over-sensitive immune system, which means their body treats certain allergens as attacks to their immune system. This results in symptoms such as itchy eyes, hives or constricted breathing as the body attempts to rid itself of the invading allergen.

People who are allergic to cats are actually allergic to a protein produced by certain glands in a cat which is present in its saliva. Cats are always licking their fur, which they then shed throughout your house. Certain breeds of cats are considered low-allergy or hypoallergenic because they either produce less of the protein that triggers allergies or their fur has properties that prevent spreading of the protein from their skin. These breeds include the Siberian, the Hairless Sphynx and the Russian Blue.

How to accommodate a person who has allergies

If you already have a furred pet such as a cat, dog or horse, there are a few things you can do to make your allergic date feel comfortable when he is visiting your home.

- Keep your bedroom off limits to your pet. No more letting your cat or hound sleep on your bed! Ensure you thoroughly clean, vacuum and air out all bedding and the mattress. If your date is worth this little sacrifice, you and your pet will soon get used to this new rule.

- Buy an air filter to extract any loose allergens in the air (cats shed skin too).

- Vacuum every couple of days—and on the day you're expecting a visit from your date. If your vacuum cleaner isn't great, you may want to upgrade to one designed to accommodate allergies, including vacuuming animal fur.

- Bathe your dog or cat at least once a month. Cats don't usually need a bath, but if you're dating someone who has a cat allergy, then it's a good idea to bathe your cat regularly. Just remember to use a shampoo designed for cats as human shampoo will irritate their skin (we have a different skin pH to animals).

- Keep all pet gear confined to one area, preferably out of the way, such as the laundry. Similarly, all used clothing should be kept confined in tubs or baskets in the laundry until it can be washed, rather than left lying out or hanging over furniture.
- Brush your dog or cat regularly to help reduce shedding
- Wash your hands and change into freshly laundered clothes before your date arrives (or before you go see him), just to be sure you've removed any allergens that may be on your hands or clothing after patting your beloved furry friend.
- Keep anti-histamine medication on hand. It may be that even with your best efforts, a reaction is triggered. Some people's immune systems may improve with exposure, and therefore their tolerance for pets may increase. For most sufferers this is not the case, and their reactions become more extreme over time. Allergies can be very serious, even life-threatening. Ensure you are well-informed about the seriousness of your date's allergies. While responsibility falls to him to ensure he has access to appropriate anti-histamine medication as recommended by a pharmacist or prescribed by a doctor, it is sound practice to make yourself aware of this as well. For example, if your date carries an epi-pen, it would be useful for you to know where it is.
- Remember, it's important you have medical advice if you or your date suffers serious allergies.

LEARNINGS FROM TINDERELLA AND JOE:

1. Be open to learning and enjoying new experiences through the dating process. You will meet guys who have various inter-

ests, such as Joe's interest in the spirit world, giving you a great opportunity to expand your horizons.

2. No-one is a mind reader. If your date has an allergy he hasn't told you about, you are not responsible if something you do, have, or cook for him gives him an allergic reaction.

3. If you own pets and he is allergic to them, work together to see if you can accommodate his allergy. If he has a life-threatening allergy, or it becomes increasingly severe over time, it may come down to him or the pet. This isn't an easy situation, but you'll need to consider it if he's proving to be someone you want to share your life with.

Chapter 12

Gary

Those who enter through the back door can expect to be shown out the window.

- Aesop

Gary was the shopping centre manager at Tinderella's workplace. He had actually approached Tinderella the old-fashioned way, in person, and by virtue of his charm and gentle persistence wooed her into going on a date.

She knew dating a co-tenant, co-worker or close friend always came with an element of risk, but surely the odds were at least 50/50? They had chatted with one another around the centre over the last couple of years, so he was familiar, and they'd developed a level of trust, which helped. Sometimes, gathering her nerve to go out with someone new was tiring. Gary had always been well mannered and kind to her, and that finally convinced Tinderella it would be okay to date him.

She also decided it was timely for her to buy a new, date worthy outfit that was different from her usual style at work, to help her feel fresh and excited for their date.

The big night rolled around and Tinderella felt a little mix of nervousness and apprehension. This was so different from meeting a new face. Gary was real. He had a connection to the world she lived and worked in every day and it was important she deal with this date with caution. To mark the occasion, she'd found the prettiest mocha-coloured dress that was a mix of feminine innocence with a touch of cheeky and she felt very comfortable in it. The fabric hugged her in a way that showed off her feminine curves but still left a little to the imagination. It was perfect. She wanted to present a different version of herself to Gary. This wasn't just another day at work, and she wanted him to look at her through fresh eyes and see a different side to her. She polished her beautiful waterhole bracelet until it gleamed and clasped it around her wrist. Looking at her reflection in the mirror, she was happy with the final result. Her phone dinged and broke into her thoughts. Gary was here!

He was waiting in the off street parking as planned. As she gathered her things she realised the wine she'd had while getting ready had started to go to her head and she was feeling a little tipsy. At least the nervousness had passed, and she was relaxed, ready to meet her date. She waved goodbye to her kids and locked the front door behind her.

Tinderella immediately saw Gary's black shiny car. She hadn't realised he had such a lovely car and was secretly pleased he'd offered to pick her up. It was the latest model V8, with twin sports exhausts and lowered. Tinderella almost drooled at the thought of this vehicle driving down the curved mountain-side to the coast. It had all the bells and whistles – an absolutely beautiful car with seat warmers and the seat instantly adjusted to her body when she sat in it.

Tinderella giggled as she greeted him, saying: 'I didn't pick you for a V8 owner.'

She had gone for a spray tan the night before, as her long legs would be on show in her new dress. She noticed that Gary showed plenty of interest in her summery glow, his eyes scanning her from top to toe as he leant in to kiss her on the cheek. He commented, tongue in cheek, that she should have waited for him to open the door for her.

She smiled in response. 'Next time.'

The drive to the lakeside yacht club was very relaxed. They chatted easily about work, which was a great icebreaker. On their arrival, the waiter showed them to their table, which was by a large, open window. It had a wonderful view of the lake, with yachts on the water and mountains in the background. The sun had just started to set, and the sky was alive with a kaleidoscope of oranges, reds and yellows, reflected on the sparkling surface of the water below. It was a picture perfect setting that could easily be framed and hung on the wall.

The conversation continued to flow, and it was lovely to see Gary was asking Tinderella questions in an effort to get to know the real her. She was enjoying the opportunity to get to know more about him, in turn.

Dinner was a luxurious experience with each course prepared to the quality of this three-star restaurant, measured by the Michelin star system, meaning "exceptional cuisine that is worth a special journey". They were served a degustation menu of the chef's signature dishes, a new experience for Tinderella. There were six delicious courses. Each dish was served with a suitably matched wine which brought out the beautiful flavour of the masterfully prepared courses. Tinderella felt a little overwhelmed by the experience—and then dessert was delivered in an elaborate glass display box. It was a work of art, with shards of meringue, caramel fondant and sugarcane slices. It literally looked too good to eat.

Gary was the first to take a slice of meringue and he let it dissolve delicately in his mouth. It was a very kissable mouth, with perfect, plump and inviting lips. Tinderella felt herself blush as she realised she was actually staring at his lips as he enjoyed the sweet dessert. She quickly looked away. She couldn't imagine what the dinner had cost, but it was one of her most lavish experiences, and one she would always remember.

Gary asked her if she was interested in having a nightcap at his house and she agreed. Why burst the bubble? Yes, she would go to Gary's place and spend some more time with him. He was a creative thinker and his complicated brain was full of ideas. Tinderella wanted to hear more.

They arrived at his house and Tinderella gasped. This wasn't a house—it was a mansion on steroids, set high on a hill with views all over the city! She had no idea Gary lived such a life of luxury and she began to feel self-conscious about her own humble home, even though it was furnished with love and warmth. Stop comparing, she told herself as Gary drove his car through the automatic gates and into the large four-car garage. There were two other cars, three motorbikes, and several hi-tech bicycles hung on custom-made racks anchored to the wall.

Gary saw Tinderella's look of disbelief on her face and he had to laugh.

'I come from very old money,' he told her. 'My father was one of the first property tycoons in the country. He was a hardworking immigrant who came to Australia with very little in his pocket, but he ended up a self-made multi-millionaire. This allows our family to live like we do. He passed away eight years ago, and I was left in a very good position.'

Gary parked the car and shrugged. 'I work because it interests me, and it keeps me grounded. Running a property investment portfolio can be quite a solitary life. Working at the office in the shopping centre I own helps me create balance and lets me connect with people. I get to know my tenant community.'

Tinderella nodded, reflecting on what he had said. This man has a few aces up his sleeve, she thought, and he obviously didn't like to show all of them at once.

Gary walked around the car to let her out of her seat as Tinderella hadn't yet moved an inch. She was still trying to take it all in. And possibly in shock, she laughed to herself. She could understand it must be a challenge for someone as well off as Gary, as others would likely judge him by his financial status and not necessarily see him for who he really was. She actually felt a little sorry for him and gave him a little hug on stepping out of his car.

Gary closed the door behind her and took her hand to guide her inside.

The house was magnificent, with high ceilings and a stunning seven-tier crystal chandelier hanging above the entry. It was an architect's dream; with a mix of old time charm and modern-day glamour.

Tinderella would never have guessed her quiet, unassuming co-worker lived in a house like this!

With a smile on his handsome face that made Tinderella focus on his beautiful plump lips again, Gary led her into a room lined wall to wall with books of all shapes and sizes. They were all leather-bound antique collectables with gold writing on the spine. Tinderella was still in awe, trying to process what she had seen, and Gary showed amused patience while he guided her over to the bar.

This must be the library, she thought. Duh! Obviously, she mocked herself.

Gary offered her a seat on an elegant bar stool and told her to relax, then walked around to the other side of the bar. He searched through the full-size fridge with clear glass doors, picking up several wine bottles and studying them until he decided on a pinot gris. Gary explained it was a grape variety of the species Vitis vinifera. Tinderella had no idea; she just knew it was white wine.

He opened the bottle and poured like a professional barman, holding the base of the bottle as he poured each glass of wine with equal amounts. He then guided Tinderella to the immaculate antique leather Chesterfield sofa and indicated for her to sit.

Time passed as they talked, and the wine seemed to disappear without her realising it. Tinderella was lost in the moment. Gary leant in to touch her face. Gently, he held her chin with his fingertips; he encouraged her to meet his gaze, to help his lips find hers.

The kiss was magical. Her heart was going into high gear, and her palms were sweating. She hardly knew where she was. Where were you hiding all this time? she thought, as his tongue gently played with her mouth. Man, this guy knew how to kiss!

Leaning back, he watched her without saying a word. Tinderella was enchanted and completely captured by his gaze, by his presence, and by his kiss. Slowly, she nodded.

Gary took her hand, then walked her to the stairwell below the beautiful chandelier. They climbed the stairs together, and he placed his hand on the small of her back to help her feel safe as she neared the top. He was a gentleman, courteous and protective of her. There was a long hallway to the left of the landing and a smaller hallway to the right that curved around toward the back of the property. Gary led Tinderella to his room at the end of the curved hallway. It was the size of three bedrooms; actually, it was the size of the whole living area in her house! The furnishings were beautiful, modern with a twist of old charm. The interior designer should be awarded a medal for this room alone, Tinderella thought. It's divine!

He led her to the large circular bed. The bed linen was so soft to touch, and he told her it was made from silk ordered especially from Singapore. If Gary wasn't so pleasant and down to earth, Tinderella would have thought he was a douche, spoilt and privileged! But his comments were said without ego. He didn't need to show off; he was who he was. Gary was rich, good looking and humble. A hat trick in one!

Had Tinderella finally found her man?

Not because of his assets, but because of the way he treated her, and the hidden depths to his mind and spirit. He obviously cared for her and wanted to know more about her. Tinderella was excited.

When he started to remove her clothing, his moves were so smooth and delicate Tinderella didn't even feel her dress released from her body. It crumpled to the floor and Gary picked her up and placed her gently on the bed. He gazed down at her and started to remove his jacket, then his shirt, and laid them with rehearsed expertise on the valet stand.

He climbed onto the bed and began to seduce Tinderella with his hands, his lips and his body. She was tingling all over and surrendered to his touch. He was a skilled lover and knew how to navigate a woman's body. His touch was electric, and his tongue was masterful at finding the right places to thrill his lover. Tinderella was on the verge of ecstasy and it showed in her body's responses to Gary's charismatic style of seduction.

Slowly he directed himself inside her, and Tinderella's whole body began to spasm with delight. Trapped within the experience, she surrendered to it. She was moments away from an intense orgasm and she could stay silent no longer. She allowed breathless noises of pleasure to escape her, noises that seemed to excite Gary, and he continued to slowly thrust inside her.

The lovemaking was almost at its peak and the bed was beginning to feel her wetness. Gary is amazing, she thought. This was exactly what she needed—a release, a moment where it was all about her and her needs. Gary indicated he wanted to change positions. Tinderella obliged and was soon in the centre of the bed on her hands and knees. It had been a while since a man had taken her from behind. Gary slowly entered her again and Tinderella moaned with pleasure, enjoying his manhood, taking in every inch of his long, thick member.

The pace changed and Gary thrust into her faster and faster. Tinderella was an eager participant, and she was ready to reach climax again. He was pumping Tinderella hard, in a sexual trance, when the unthinkable happened. His manhood slipped into her anus.

Oh my God!

The size and width of Gary's member was far too much for Tinderella's butt-hole to bear. The pain it caused was more than she could handle. She had never had anal sex before and this was far from the ideal introduction to it.

Tinderella fainted.

She literally passed out on the bed from the pain. Time stood still. Later, Tinderella would piece together what happened next. Gary was at a loss. He had no idea what to do as he had never experienced this before! He instantly apologised when he saw Tinderella's reaction, although she couldn't hear him as she was still out cold. It was an obvious accident, and Gary was embarrassed and shocked at what had happened. He gently rolled her over and covered her with the bed sheet, then patted her cheek repeatedly to wake her. When that failed, he quickly ran to the bathroom to find a washer to dampen her face in an effort to revive her. He knew he would have to call an ambulance if she didn't wake. He truly didn't know what else to do.

The gentle tapping, kind words and wet washer helped Tinderella regain consciousness. Her eyes fluttered, and she woke up with the realisation of the recent event in her head, and oh! The pain! After a moment, she was able to look at Gary and could see his concern, embarrassment and regret. He was genuinely worried. The poor man, Tinderella thought. Then waves of extreme embarrassment swamped her, and she knew she had to go. She couldn't look at him anymore. She had to leave! In truth, she was completely unsure of how to deal with this. Her face was getting hot, and she knew it was turning a bright shade of beetroot. She just had to get out of there and hide!

She quickly gathered her things and scurried to the bathroom to get dressed, staying in there as she arranged an Uber to pick her up.

Somehow, she finished dressing. She thanked Gary and apologised to him while walking out of his bedroom very fast and fled out the front door. She left Gary standing in the middle of his magnificent room with a look of complete bewilderment on his face.

Tinderella was soon in the Uber and breathed a huge sigh of relief. She was going home to her safe place. It was where she needed to be. Oh, the embarrassment! She cried silently on the trip home. She was so upset and ashamed over what had just occurred.

Days later, Gary had tried to find a quiet space to talk to Tinderella, but she was avoiding him at all costs. She was still so embarrassed, and she couldn't face him. It was too much for her to bear. She saw him around the shopping centre often, and she could cope with that—as long as he kept his distance. The last thing she needed was for the centre's grapevine to hear the gossip she had passed out having anal sex!

Why, oh why did I date a guy that works so close? she asked herself over and over again.

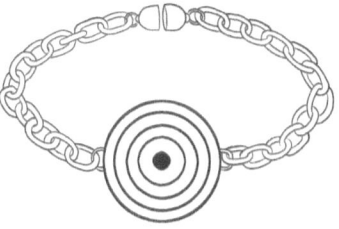

It's Time to Talk... by Simone

DEALING WITH A WORKPLACE ROMANCE

It pays to be cautious about dating someone who is a professional colleague, co-worker or connected in some way through your job or business. Tinderella definitely took a risk by dating someone in the same workplace. Understandably, it's not an uncommon situation. Most of us will spend the majority of our life at work. Over time, you can get to know people quite well through your job or your business (at least in a work sense). These connections can sometimes develop into romantic or sexual attractions—and at times, happy relationships.

Some workplaces actively discourage office romances, and some of us may choose not to act on an initial attraction even if we can, being all too aware of the downsides if a romance fails. If you find you are becoming attracted to someone at work, you need to check in on a few things first.

Office romance checklist
- Ask yourself whether this is just a crush or if you do genuinely have feelings for this guy you would like to explore.
- Consider the consequences if things don't go as well as you hope. This is very likely to have an impact not only on your career or business but on his as well. Be sure you are prepared to take that risk.
- If you do wish to ask him out, or agree to his request for a date, then ask yourself if you will feel comfortable seeing him again the next day at work if your first date with him is a flop. Equally, are you prepared to be rejected by the guy if you ask him out and he declines? Can you cope with the awkwardness if your feelings are not mutual, when you may be bumping into him daily in the tea room or having to work with him on a project?

- If your first date is a success and you want to see him again, it's important you find out how he feels about dating someone so closely connected to his workplace, and also the consequences if things don't work out. It's a discussion you both need to have before taking that next step of exploring a potential relationship or even just a sexual dalliance, which involves a sexual relationship that is not lasting or serious.
- If he works for the same employer or even in the same industry as you, do you need to let your manager(s) or employer(s) know about it? Are there rules in your organisation that forbid office relationships? Does this relationship create a possible or actual conflict of interest?
- Consider whether you want to keep things private and not let your other colleagues or managers know, or if so, when you want that to happen—right away, or when your relationship is more established? Have this conversation with the guy you're interested in to make sure you are in agreement on this. New relationships are favourite fodder around the water cooler!

Look for a balance between work and play

Colleagues who date usually have a mutual interest in the work they do together. If they're in different parts of the same organisation, they are likely to have shared views or opinions about their employer. If they work for different organisations in the same industry, or which have a professional connection, or in their own businesses which then trade services, they are likely to have shared professional interests.

It's important to explore each other's personal interests, hobbies and values outside of your working relationship. These have the potential to enrich your relationship, and equally may negatively affect it. Make sure there's scope for growth, because once you're in a relationship you'll be spending a LOT of time together.

Be aware of the power balance in a relationship

Gary's riches made Tinderella feel a little uneasy. It's certainly not every day you meet someone who has extraordinary wealth. It's a common perception in today's world that money equals power. When one person in a relationship earns significantly more than the other, or holds a position of seniority above (or even directly over) the other, there can be a subconscious shift of power to the higher earner/senior position holder. This can create tensions and become an underlying cause of arguments, for example, the man expecting the woman to do all the childcare because her job is less senior or 'important' than his. Such an imbalance of power can be unsettling, especially for women who value their hard-won independence. If the woman is the higher earner, some men may feel uncomfortable (consciously or subconsciously) if they perceive themselves as the primary breadwinner. Understandably, no one wants to feel 'less than' their partner in any way.

Remember, money or job status does not define a person or their worth, nor does it truly measure the balance in a relationship.

AN INTRODUCTION TO ANAL SEX

Anal sex is not for everyone, but plenty of women enjoy it. Sex is, of course, meant to be pleasurable, and definitions of pleasure differ from person to person, as do the things that arouse us. Some love it, some don't. Men who love it say anal sex feels tighter and therefore extremely pleasurable. Some men also see anal sex as a form of assertiveness, dominance and power, especially if they can pressure the woman into 'consenting' to anal sex at their request. Women who love it say it feels adventurous. Some even report achieving more intense orgasms through anal sex, particularly when preceded by vaginal orgasms.

While pop culture saw 2014 declared the year of the booty, anal sex is still regarded as taboo by many. The internet offers sound information about anal sex, and education is the best way to make sure that no one is having anal sex if they don't want to, and if they do, the experience is a safe and positive one.

Consent is still required. Being 'sexually adventurous' or 'sex positive' does not equal 'always down for anything', and it is always your choice if you have anal sex. Most bad first experiences are due to feeling pressured into it, moving too fast, not using enough lubrication, or the expectation anal sex must involve deep penetration, when in fact external stimulation and light, shallow penetration is ideal for accessing the high concentration of nerve endings around and just inside the anus.

The penis accidentally slipping into the anus is not uncommon when having vaginal sex—and can sometimes be an excuse by guys to try anal sex without your consent, but as Tinderella experienced, this tends to be extremely painful. Fainting as Tinderella did is not uncommon either, as sudden pain and shock can cause a person's heart rate and blood pressure to drop suddenly, interrupting the flow of blood to the brain...

Prepping for anal sex

The best way to avoid being woken by an ambulance officer standing over your naked self is to ensure your guy helps you to feel super relaxed, and you are well lubricated before entry. Gentleness, plenty of lubrication, and good communication is key.

The butt does not self-lubricate, and this is a very sensitive area of the body, which can also tear easily. Shop carefully for your lubrication of choice, as there are several types available, and not all are compatible with sex toys or condoms. The more lube the better, as this makes penetration easier and more enjoyable.

The muscles in your anus are designed to push downwards and outwards and are particularly strong. Put simply, this part of your body is designed to 'expel' not 'welcome in'. Relaxing these muscles involves relaxing you generally, followed by gentle and slow penetration by the guy. Your partner can use his finger(s) first to 'open' you, and butt plugs are another option. These come in various sizes. They are designed to be inserted into the anus for a period of time before sex to ensure the inner ring of muscle is genuinely relaxed enough to avoid pain from anal sex. Once it is inside, the body will accept this foreign intrusion and then the true enjoyment for you both can begin.

We've all been socialised to believe the butt is a dirty place, so be aware of this conditioning and remember you can take steps to prepare yourself for anal sex by practising basic hygiene, just as you would for any other sexual activity. This can include having a poo first and showering to wash the area thoroughly. Note that it's normal to see some traces of poo during anal sex.

And do remember to use condoms (on any sex toys as well), as it is possible to contract STIs through anal sex.

Learnings from Tinderella and Gary:

1. Always think twice about dating a guy who you work with. The consequences can be very uncomfortable—or even career altering—if things don't work out.

2. Imbalances in income or seniority may make you or your partner feel uncomfortable (even if it is at a subconscious level) if you feel that there is also a power imbalance. If this is an issue for you, then recognise it for what it is before things proceed any further, so you address and discuss this together to ensure balance in your relationship is achieved in other ways.

3. Anal sex can be pleasurable but is always your choice. If you are open to and agree to the experience, then make sure you are physically well prepared for anal penetration.

Chapter 13

Steve

Sometimes… sometimes our hearts… crack a little.

- Brodi Ashton

There was a definite connection between Steve and Tinderella from the moment they laid eyes on each other. He was sitting at a table in the far corner of the bar with his head down, looking at his phone. Tinderella walked towards him, and that's when the magic happened.

Steve looked up, their eyes locked, and their energies connected. It felt as though someone had plugged her into an invisible electrical current, jolting her with a powerful zap of ecstasy. This was huge, a significant sign to Tinderella, and she lost her breath for a minute.

Steve rose to greet her. His hand slipped to hold her hip just below her waist as he leant in and kissed her on the cheek, close to her mouth. His kiss was confident, his lips warm, and his slightly unshaven face felt rough and invigorating against her skin. The man could have been a model. He was tall, about 6'2", with a lean muscular body—just the kind Tinderella lusted after. His ruggedly handsome face lit up when he smiled, and he had an easy manner about him that made her comfortable. She was instantly attracted to him and was keen to see how things would unfold.

She had worn her favourite piece of clothing, a short floral jumpsuit. It was so comfortable, and she looked fabulous in it. The fabric was soft and flattered the silhouette of her body. It was a casual jumpsuit, but her chocolate stilettos, classic cowhide clutch and beloved silver waterhole bracelet added wow factor. She had styled her hair with a product from an organic Australian brand. She loved the result — and her hair smelled divine!

Steve was, in fact, the perfect height for Tinderella when she was wearing her stilettos—she fitted into his arms just right. She was a lover of shoes and had several pairs of designer shoes, brands like Jimmy Choo, Miu Miu, and Manolo Blahnik. They were packaged with care in their original shoeboxes, kept in mint condition. She even had a list of every pair of shoes in her closet for easy access, so she was very excited at the prospect of being able to wear them more often in Steve's company. She didn't want to jinx it, so she tried to clear her mind and focus on the man in front of her.

And he was a delicious specimen. Steve was an entrepreneur, and he was passionate about his business ventures, showing her many photos on his phone from current and past projects. These included pieces he had made with his own hands. Seeing a man so gifted at doing creative projects as well as manual labour really turned her on.

Oh, close my legs! she thought, trying to discipline her lustful brain and resist the urge to touch him.

Steve chatted away. He was clearly a deep thinker. Embarrassingly, Tinderella found herself just watching him talk; she couldn't quite focus on what he was saying, she was just watching his mouth move. He had good teeth too, always a bonus for any man.

Okay, concentrate! she told herself. She did try, but this guy was so freaking hot and the energy was sizzling! She found herself looking at his crotch. She had never done that before, but it was so full in his jeans and she so desperately wanted to see what was behind that zipper. Snapping back to reality, she quickly looked away, hoping she hadn't been caught. Tinderella was so embarrassed! Get a grip, girlfriend, she told herself.

At that moment a song started to play on the bar's audio system—George Benson's *Nothing's Gonna Change My Love For You*. Ohhhh, geez! She wanted to freeze that moment in time, place a big passionate kiss on Steve's mouth, and then unfreeze once she'd had her way with him. She wondered what his expression would be... This guy was getting her juices flowing and there was no turning that tap off.

He went to the bar to order her Long Island Iced Tea, and she was secretly relieved to have a break from sitting so close to him so she could regain her composure and calm down. She watched him walk to the bar, following his every move. He was truly tasty—edible, even. Tinderella wanted to spend many many hours discovering and devouring him and... she stopped herself—wow, this was bad! Her heart was already skipping along to a new song. Could love at first sight be real? Or was this lust? Oh, who really cares! Tinderella was on heat. She just wanted Steve to pull his shirt off and allow her to ravage his body...

Okay—stop, she told herself.

Steve returned to the table, drinks in hand, and carefully placed them on the coasters. Tinderella was impressed he was so well housetrained. So many men seemed to lack basic household etiquette. What was it with the toilet seat left up, the dirty cup in the sink, the undies on the floor? But was she being too petty? No. Tinderella was mesmerised. She could already see a future with this man and her imagination started to run wild. She pictured the perfect beach wedding, complete with beautiful white flowers and a solo guitarist strumming as she walked down the aisle. Her future was set, and it looked to be a very happy one.

Tinderella zoned back into the conversation. Steve was telling her about his past days as a drummer in a band, which had gained a reputable following. She finished her drink. It was time to leave the bar and get her hands on this magnificent creature. She asked Steve if he was able to drive her home. He obliged. He was so hospitable!

They arrived at her home and she could feel Steve standing behind her as she reached for her keys. His energy was warm and inviting. Tinderella did her best to remain calm and guided him into her main living area. The décor was ultra modern, although warm, with splashes of modern art that captured the eye of every visitor. The large painting hanging on the wall over the gas fireplace mesmerised Steve. It was an absorbing native Indigenous piece in full colour Tinderella had purchased on her recent visit to Arnhem Land.

He walked toward her and drew her close, then held her chin with his fingers, gently raising her head toward him. He angled his face to hers and began to kiss her with his warm, open mouth. He was finding her soul in the kiss, but she was lost. Tinderella was in a place she had never been before. It was the first time she had felt so vulnerable in love. Wow, she thought. Is that what it feels like?

Was Steve showing a true interest in her?

Had Tinderella been able to capture his attention in this short time?

She was certainly wishing it was so. Steve would fit into her world perfectly with his rugged charm and his smooth ability to communicate. This alone was beyond her expectations of any guy. He could talk! He could hold a conversation! He was the complete answer to Tinderella's vision board of the perfect guy.

Steve walked her into the kitchen and lifted her onto the bench. He was kissing her neck, and she shuddered with pleasure at his touch, arching her back in pure delight.

The connection felt perfect on every level—emotional, physical and mental. It was the perfect triangle. Was this her forever fairy tale? Her potential soul mate, the guy she wanted to grow old with?

Steve kissed her long and hard on the mouth and thanked her for being so beautiful.

Tinderella's heart melted, and she snuggled into his masculine chest. She felt a connection with him she had never experienced with other lovers. She could finally remove herself from the dating sites she had joined because in her mind, she had found the man of her dreams, and she wasn't about to jeopardise this newfound relationship. This was the connection she had been searching for all her life.

Tinderella was happy to be held by her new man and became lost in his eyes for the hundredth time. He removed her jumpsuit and his tongue began to play with her erect nipples as they tightened in response. He ran his left hand up her leg, to her thigh, and her tiny lace knickers. Tinderella gasped when Steve's fingers started to slide them to the side for him to have his way with her. He reached into his pocket to pull out a small packet and slid a condom onto his swollen manhood. Safe sex was a definite priority, and she happily allowed him time to prepare himself. Steve was well practiced at this and it didn't interfere with the momentum or the mood. He pulled her closer; he was the perfect height to penetrate her easily. He slid into her and her body responded instantly with a welcoming wetness.

Steve pulled her toward him and tugged on her hair firmly but gently, his fingers sliding over her scalp. Tinderella had had experienced lovers before, but Steve had a sense of control that showed his skill in the art of lovemaking. Staying inside her, he carried her to the thick pile rug on the floor in the lounge room and made passionate love to her. He touched her body delicately all over, taking her to the brink of insanity. It seemed to last a lifetime and Tinderella was able to reach climax several times. He then laid her on her back and confidently positioned his head between her legs, expertly stimulating her clitoris. She came with a force she had never felt before. Steve climbed above her and penetrated her, breathing hard. As he came he shuddered in pleasure. Their lovemaking was complete, and they were exhausted. They stayed in each other's arms, watching the fire and savouring the moment.

Steve kissed her on the forehead and asked where the bathroom was; he needed to remove the condom and refresh. Tinderella showed him to her small bathroom with its retro style fixtures. He noticed the old-style bath and commented that next time he would take her in the bath, then sponge her all over. Tinderella was so happy. This was a place she hadn't been in a long time.

She left him to do what he needed to do and walked naked to the kitchen. She opened a bottle of pinot gris and poured two glasses. Steve entered the room, naked and relaxed, clearly confident with his body. Seriously, why shouldn't he be? The results of his days at the gym were clear to see. He sat at the counter and looked into Tinderella's eyes. His expression was different, one she couldn't explain. What was he thinking? The mood had changed.

Steve cleared his throat. 'Tinderella, I have something to tell you,' he said, low and cautious. 'I've never met a woman I'm so attracted to, in every way.'

Tinderella blushed and, hiding her nervousness, took a big sip of her wine.

'But,' he continued.

Uh oh! Tinderella started to panic. What but? They had just experienced the most amazing night of lovemaking and now there was a 'but'?

And then the blow fell.

Steve explained he was in a loveless marriage. He had travelled to Bali and met a local girl. They'd had a short but lustful week together. 'Completely innocent and in the mode of holiday fun,' he said. They had experienced days of sex and passion until he left her to move onto his next destination. He looked Tinderella in the eyes as he told her the girl had fallen pregnant. He had brought her to Australia and married her. These events were out of his control. His new partner spoke very little English, and he felt committed to her through his responsibility to their child and her lack of understanding of this new and foreign country. Steve told Tinderella he felt guilt and responsibility for his child, who was only young. He needed to be there for them both as a father and husband, at least until they became self-sufficient, which could be many years away.

They could never see each other again.

Tinderella felt sick—almost as if she really was going to vomit. Bile rose in her throat and it was as bitter as the news she had just heard from this man sitting naked in front of her. She had no words. He had used her, taken her in his arms like he was invested in her, in their future together, and then betrayed her confidence.

Steve walked toward her to hug her. Tinderella pulled away and told him he had to go, to leave now. Get out.

This could not be happening.

Every hope-filled thought about this man was now in ashes.

Tinderella watched as Steve gathered his belongings, dressed and walked out the door.

The bile that had parked in her throat now had to come up. She rushed into the bathroom and leant over the toilet. Tinderella's body shuddered violently through each spasm.

Her tears started to flow. He had seduced her and lied to her. He was a player, and cunning at that. Tinderella sat on the cold floor and cried, her throat burning with acid. Was her life never going to become what she wanted? She didn't desperately need a man… but she wanted one. A man she could share fun times and life experiences with, and they would be there for each other.

Steve was obviously not after what he had previously alluded to. Tinderella was just a plaything with which he could manipulate to satisfy his sexual cravings.

She got angry, cursing his name through her convulsing tears and hoping he would one day feel a small degree of the pain she was feeling. If he had told her upfront he was in a marriage of convenience and committed to his international bride, she would have accepted that. The night could have possibly played out in a different way, with both of them being aware of the reality of it all. But Steve had withheld the truth, used her and cast her aside, only minutes after he had been inside her.

She was empty, much like her heart, her soul and her life. She wiped her face, blew her nose and climbed in to bed to hide her shame from the world, sick and numb over the night's events. She'd had no warning Steve would treat her as a commodity. She felt violated; it was sex under false pretences. This was the last time any man would fool her that way, she vowed. Hot tears still burnt her face. She needed sleep. Her emotions had taken over her mind and let her imagine her future, but all she had created was a false reality. Tinderella promised herself she would never let this happen again and drifted off to a troubled sleep, sobbing and broken.

She was alone.

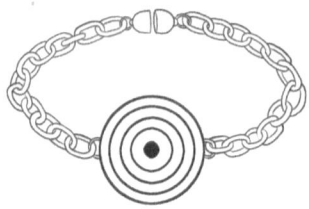

It's Time to Talk... by Simone

DEALING WITH DATING APP CHEATERS

Online dating sites are rife with men who are miserable in their marriages or long-term relationships and looking to feel wanted, or who just want a fling behind their partner's back. These men rarely share their intent with the women they are dating for fear of being found out by their partners. A 2015 survey conducted by the consumer profiling company, GlobalWebIndex[13] indicated 4 in 10 people who use Tinder are already in a relationship. One third of those people are actually married. No wonder people are wary of online dating sites!

Some guys will state up front in their profile description they are in a long-term relationship and just looking for fun on the side. It's not so easy to pick the guys who are married and want to hide that important detail. Remember to do your due diligence and look for some of the most common telltale signs.

Men already in a committed relationship and looking for a dalliance on the sly may not post photos of their face. Instead, they'll post photos of their dog, or foreign places they've visited (and they are not present in the actual photos). Their profile photos may be taken in such a way you can't quite make out their faces, or they upload photos of their bare chests with their head slightly cut out of the photo. This type of 'mysterious' profile should be treated as a red flag by women seeking love rather than just sex.

Note the GlobalWebIndex survey did not give a breakdown of how many of those married Tinder users were male, and how many female. Women are also online looking for dalliances or distractions outside of their relationships... perhaps we may yet get to read the *Tales of Tinderfella*.

---

[13] https://blog.globalwebindex.com/trends/what-to-know-about-tinder/

Why do people cheat?

There are many reasons people cheat. Steve, for example, may have cheated because he was angry at his wife for tying him to her with an unwanted pregnancy. Some of the most common reasons include:

- Blame: it's my work's fault (I'm so stressed); it's my wife's fault (she's neglectful, too fat); it's my health (depression)
- Denial: my mates do it so it's okay; it's not really cheating if it's a blow job
- Escapism: from responsibilities of life; from a loveless marriage; from fear of intimacy
- Addiction: addicted to sex; addicted to the thrill of deceit; addicted to drugs/alcohol that impair judgement and self-control
- Self-gratification: selfish attitude to own needs and wants; sense of entitlement to sex (if she won't give it to me, then I'll go elsewhere); ego-based narcissistic tendencies

Regardless of what needs a cheater is seeking to meet, his actions often have a devastating impact on the unsuspecting women he connects with. As Tinderella shared in her story, when Steve withheld the truth, it made her vulnerable by setting false expectations and manipulating her choices in his favour.

Where do the cheaters lurk?

Perhaps an indicator of a subscriber's true intentions in their search for sex, friendship or marriage can be found in the tag lines of which popular dating apps they choose:

- Tinder: Meet new and interesting people nearby
- Plenty of Fish: Helping single people all over the world converse and connect

- e-Harmony: Making more meaningful connections that lead to fulfilling marriages
- RSVP: Find a keeper

At least the dating apps are more upfront about their mission and services than some of their subscribers. The relative anonymity and lack of accountability online means people can and do lie on their dating profiles. Although some sites are perceived as more relationship-focused than others, it's wisest not to make assumptions. You may come across people on 'marriage-making' sites who are just after untethered sex, while others meet their long-term partner on casual hook-up sites. Always do your due diligence.

The trends of user experiences on dating sites shift over time, and there are always new apps entering the market. Dating sites are big business! Most dating apps have been designed by men and offer little to deter bad behaviour by male users (sending dick pics, texting pornographic messages, lying about their relationship status), which reflects the less attractive side of the sex-focused hook-up culture some apps are known for.

Women are starting to be recognised as a consumer force in their own right when it comes to online dating, and the market has responded with an array of woman-friendly apps. Consider some of the newer options such as Bumble, Happn or The League.

THE TRUTH ABOUT LOVE AT FIRST SIGHT

Falling in love is a magical feeling. Tinderella felt she had connected with Steve on every level—emotionally, physically and mentally. When we 'fall in love' it is a whole body experience.

- When we meet someone we're attracted to, our body produces more of the feel-good chemical phenylethylamine, which in turn helps to produce higher levels of dopamine—the neurotransmitter that lights up our brain's reward centre. Phenylethylamine is found naturally in chocolate, which is why chocolate also makes you feel good.

- Release of the stress hormones cortisol and adrenaline increases, causing us to feel physical sensations such as 'butterflies in the stomach', sweaty palms and feeling our hearts 'skip a beat'.

- The hormone oxytocin is released through physical touch with your lover and creates feelings of happiness and euphoria.

- When we are in love we produce less serotonin, a chemical used to transmit messages between nerve cells. This reduction in serotonin causes a person to feel obsessed with their new love. Interestingly, having low levels of serotonin is common in people who have obsessive compulsive disorder.

This means when we fall in love with someone, we feel euphoric but also anxious at the same time, and we become a little 'obsessed' with our new love and want to see him as much as possible.

How to keep your emotions and thoughts in check

When you consider what's happening physically as you fall in love, with all those hormones and biochemical interactions flooding your body, you can understand why it sometimes feels your emotions have run away from you, your heart is overriding your head, and your imagination has run amok.

Being in love is an addictive feeling. It makes it easy to overlook things in a person who will potentially burst that bubble of euphoria down the track, hence the phrase 'blinded by love'.

Yet Tinderella's reaction to Steve was not just a physical and emotional reaction. It was her imagination that instantly came up with all the detailed scenarios (planning her wedding; seeing Steve fit perfectly into her world) that created such high expectations in her and made the rejection at the end of their night together so much more painful for her.

It's only natural to get excited when we meet someone who seems to tick a lot of our boxes. The reason why we write this list in the first place is to help us to imagine our lives with our ideal partner and what that looks and feels like. Our imagination then does a great job filling our minds with the possibilities of a future when we meet a fabulous new guy. But it's important to rein in your imagination after the first date, the first sexual encounter, the first morning after... until we get a lot further along than these few 'firsts'. As in the movie *How to lose a guy in 10 days*, when one person races too far ahead of the other too quickly, it can actually smother the relationship before it begins. There is also a risk the person you are dating will turn out to not be who you thought they were. It takes time to get to know someone.

There are plenty of times when you want your imagination to run wild, for example, when you're brainstorming for a project. But it's important to be able to 'get a grip' in the moment and not let your imagination run too far away with you in the early stages of dating. Even though our body is pulsing with hormones and biochemicals, we can govern our thoughts, which will in turn guide our emotions, and we can choose our behaviours—at least until you have established trust and a deeper connection.

Balanced thinking checklist
- Make a list of what you like/don't like about this guy so you don't overlook or minimise those traits you wouldn't ordinarily accept in a potential life partner.
- If you find you are obsessively thinking about this guy, then try various enjoyable 'distractions' that keep the feel-good hormones happening within you, but which are separate to what you're experiencing with him. Balance out the things that give you joy in your life, so your feel-

good feelings are not all centred on your new guy. You can increase your natural serotonin and dopamine levels through activities such as exercise, meditation, walking in sunshine, catchups with friends, escaping to the movies and more.

- Think twice, act once. Carefully consider and filter your text and in-person conversations and actions during the early days of your budding relationship, to keep your emotions close to your chest until such time you feel comfortable to take your relationship to the next level.

- Remind yourself you have identified an extensive list of qualities and traits that are important to you, through your lived experiences and your ideals about your life, and it will take time for the guy's true qualities and traits to reveal themselves to you.

- Remind yourself taking the time to see if this guy is 'the one' is a valuable investment in yourself and your life. There are plenty of fish in the sea, and you never know who is around the corner waiting for you if this current guy doesn't end up ticking all of your boxes.

- Focus your thoughts on other areas in your life that require your energy and attention to maintain balance in your life while dating. When you're drawn to a guy, it's very easy to spend a lot of time with him on dates and outings to the detriment of other areas and commitments in your life.

- Keep your creative imagination usefully employed by planning a re-vamp of a room in your home, or a party, or designing a vegie garden or similar. Doing the physical work is then a great outlet for the adrenalin and cortisol in your body.

DEALING WITH REJECTION

It's incredibly hurtful to be rejected, perhaps even more so when it involves deception as Tinderella experienced. Being rejected by someone you are attracted to can impact on your self-esteem, your mental health, and your trust in men generally. People can experience physical symptoms too, such as difficulty sleeping or eating. Here are a few suggestions to help overcome the pain of rejection:

- Remind yourself how awesome you are! Make a list of your best traits. If you are having trouble coming up with this list, ask your girlfriends to help you.
- Make a list of all the traits you actually didn't like about the guy anyway. With every trait you add, say out loud 'Thank heavens I've dodged that bullet!'
- Hang out with people who love you and who will remind of how loved and supported you are.
- Let it go. Holding on to the pain is only hurting you more. He's already long gone! Find other people or activities that give you joy.
- If your symptoms lead to anxiety or depression, please see your doctor or a therapist for support.

LEARNINGS FROM TINDERELLA AND STEVE:

1. There will be men on dating online who are not honest about their relationship status or their intentions. They are on all dating apps—regardless of the advertised user demographics. Forewarned is forearmed when it comes to the existence of cheaters online. Beware the profile photos that omit the person's face.

2. Physical and emotional changes take place in your body when you fall in love with someone. Keep your emotions close to your chest until you've established trust with a guy and are comfortable taking things to the next level.

3. Remember, you are awesome! As the dating app says... there are indeed plenty of fish in the sea.

Chapter 14

Sam

When you don't dress like everybody else, you don't have to think like everybody else.

- Iris Apfel

Sam's an interesting one, thought Tinderella, as she sat in bed with her laptop in front of her and chatted to him online. He was very fashion aware and often mentioned his love of clothing design and fashion. He would delve into the history of fashion with her and describe in detail the way fashion had changed over the years. He marvelled at fashion's ability to influence people's shopping choices and how the consumer market would spend its money. Sam explained how a lot of research goes into the design of certain styles to make sure big companies secure a solid percentage of the market. Without these analytical research tools that help to predict and define trends, a company could see their designs fail to sell at all, causing great financial losses.

The passion in his messages about algorithms and statistical predictions was fascinating to Tinderella, and she loved reading his replies to every question she asked. He was very detailed in his responses and provided her with a new insight into the world of fashion. She was in awe of this man, who was very different in his easy manner with her then she imagined he must be in his day job as an editor for one of the largest newspapers in the country. His personality seemed to split depending on which topic they chatted about, shifting from serious senior editor to flamboyant and creative fashion guru. This intrigued Tinderella—it was the first time she had spoken to a man with almost polar opposite tastes and interests between his 'every day' self and his creative self.

Sam and Tinderella had been chatting religiously for several weeks. It was time for her to get to know him better, and the best way for that to happen was to meet him in person and connect one on one. She was waiting for Sam to make the first move, but it was like pulling hen's teeth. He would dance around the subtle hints she would put out there during their conversations, and often came back with deadlines or work and family commitments. Although he was absolutely single, and had been for many years, he was a true family man and a committed father to his two sons from his previous marriage.

Tinderella could see Sam had a level of understanding and compassion not found in many men, based on her own experience. This was the reason they continued to talk, and she often looked forward to the time on her computer chatting to Sam of an evening with her glass of wine in hand.

She learnt things about fashion she had never known before. Sam talked knowledgeably about how important it was to match each style with the correct shoe type, and even the small details such as the earrings. A misstep could take you from a fashion icon to a fashion boo-boo. As they chatted online, Tinderella would take notes in the writing pad she kept by to her; to remind her of the many priceless tips Sam gave her. She mentally noted she had made many faux pas in the past, but now, with Sam's help, she would be a woman of fashion—something she had always dreamt of. Not that Tinderella wanted to be in the spotlight all the time, but she did enjoy the odd compliment about her appearance. Sure, she wasn't Hollywood gorgeous, but she was pretty in her own way. And if she could do anything to add to that, and create a little more positive attention, she was there!

Sam's favourite movie was *The Devil Wears Prada*. He had seen it over a hundred times and thought Meryl Streep was 'a divine goddess'. He had been lucky enough to see her from afar at a media junket and had literally drooled with lust after the golden creature. Tinderella had to giggle at his fascination with the beautiful Ms.

Streep—who could blame him? Those cheekbones. That amazing acting ability. She was indeed a goddess on the big screen.

Sam would often talk about the garments in each scene of the movie, how they should have been worn and where you could source them for purchase. He often praised Miranda's fashion sense and her ability to hold herself as a true editor in control should.

Tinderella's day job as a hair stylist entailed helping her customers choose the right look for their hair, and on a very casual basis she was also a clothing store assistant. She preferred the title 'women's fashion advisor', as this gave the role the respect it—and she—deserved. It wasn't something she wanted to do forever, but it gave her a taste of something she loved to do apart from her hairdressing. The smell of newly arrived stock from the European, American or Asian markets sent tingles up her arms, a feeling she had every time a new shipment was delivered to the store. She often told Sam about the new stock arrival and he would ask her to describe it in such detail it became a game to them both, almost like a type of foreplay. Sam would respond with excited replies to Tinderella's description of each different shipment.

It was a joy to be able to share this with Sam and have another feel the excitement that she did. Maybe Sam's first kiss with her would bring the same feeling. Oh, to have him in front of her in the flesh and be able to talk to him openly about the world around them. She still had so many questions to ask him, but it was a patience game with this one.

Was it a type of courting perhaps? Sam was a bit older than the guys Tinderella had dated before. Maybe this was how the older generation did it?

So Tinderella just had to be patient, one thing she was, admittedly, very bad at.

One evening, Sam seemed very excited to chat to Tinderella about a particular wrap he had seen online. He developed messaging diarrhoea! Tinderella didn't have time to respond and the message bell was going nuts! Sam was enthralled with this piece. He spoke of where it had come from, how it was a limited edition, and the intricate detail within the hand-stitched designs. It was a piece he had to buy, even if it was destined to be a gift for just the right person. Tinderella's eyes opened wide—was Sam hinting he would buy the wrap for her?

She squealed in delight. Sam had sent her several images of the piece in question, and it was beyond stunning! The wrap was made from the finest silks in the world, spun by silkworms fed on organically grown mulberry trees. The wrap was handwoven on ancient handlooms, without electricity, and it took many months to weave each limited-edition wrap. Once woven, the wrap then had tiny Swarovski crystals handsewn into the design. After that, the finest 24-carat gold thread was stitched into the intricate pattern around the crystals. Finally, silver particles were infused onto the wrap and sealed to hold the shimmer in place. Tinderella could see why this wrap was a rarity on the fashion scene, and worthy of being a collectable.

Imagine if he is buying it for me, she thought shamelessly, but she quickly put that thought out of her head. The next time they were online, Sam confirmed he had purchased one of the wraps and it was due to arrive in the next week. He was beyond excited! It was nice to see Sam display so much enthusiasm for a piece of fashion, and Tinderella got caught up in it too. She asked him if he would like to come over and check out her wardrobe—maybe there were a few pieces he could suggest she put together, or scrap some that were really just wardrobe fillers.

He was pleasantly surprised and said he would be honoured to help her sort out her clothing dilemmas.

Tinderella put careful planning into what she would wear in front of Sam. She didn't want to make any fashion stuff ups, or have Sam be critical of her choice or even worse suggest she never wear that style again! She decided dressing casually would be best. She put on her torn light blue jeans, her fashion wedges, and her fitted white top with her white leather jacket. The jacket was a favourite, but she rarely wore it for fear of getting it marked.

She wore her waterhole bracelet as a necklace, extending it with white thin leather cords which added a uniquely different look to complete the outfit.

The night came, and by pure coincidence Sam had received his much awaited delivery that same day. Yes, his wrap had arrived, and he couldn't wait to show it to her. He told her that he would be bringing cotton gloves to hold it as he didn't want to have any natural body oils penetrate the delicate fabric. Tinderella agreed. In the back of her mind she was a little taken aback. So why had he purchased it? Was it not to be worn?

Tinderella had prepared a platter of hors d'oeuvres including blue cheese, a variety of dips and imported prosciutto. She accompanied it with a sparkling wine recommended by the salesman at the liquor store. She wanted tonight to be welcoming for Sam, relaxed and fun. She hoped he would be impressed with her entertaining style and find her attractive and desirable through the subtle hints she planned to 'put out' this evening. Sam was due to arrive. She had asked her friend Sarah to call her in exactly forty minutes to check on her safety and to see if the night was starting well. She would then tell Sarah whether to call her again in an hour or so and keep tabs on her throughout the night. Tinderella hadn't met Sam in the flesh as yet, but she had researched him and the details he'd given about his current job and where he lived were authentic. Still, she wasn't going to take any chances.

The doorbell rang, and Tinderella opened the door.

Sam was smaller than she had expected. Her first thoughts were he could almost pass as a jockey. It wasn't one of her finest moments as Sam must have sensed her apprehension and said, 'Good things come in small packages!'

This was the perfect icebreaker as Tinderella replied, 'Of course they do!'

She invited him into her home and thanked him for coming over to help her reorganize her closet. Sam had freshly showered and had a cleanliness about him that was almost sterile. It had been a while since Tinderella had seen a guy so well scrubbed he nearly reflected the lighting in her hallway! He had a box in his arms, the most beautiful she had ever seen. It was covered in gorgeous fabric and embossed with a name—Samuel Cowen. It was Sam's full name, and he smiled with glee as he looked at the stunning personalised package. Tinderella could tell he was ready to show her what was inside.

She invited him into the kitchen area, the heart of the home and where the entertaining took place. Sam took a seat at the breakfast bar and placed the box on the stool next to him, away from the food Tinderella had laid out. The care she had taken in providing him with a chic and hospitable welcome clearly impressed him.

Tinderella handed him the bottle of wine so he could open it for them. He poured the wine and handed her her glass. Together they toasted to each other's success, with Sam adding he hoped he wouldn't find any fashion disasters in Tinderella's closet. They laughed and drank the sweetness down. After nibbles and giggles, they decided to take the party to Tinderella's closet. Sam followed her into her bedroom, then handed her his glass and made a beeline for her closet. She laughed at his reaction—he was like a child in a candy store at Christmas.

Sam began with the dresses, and his face was an open book. For some he raised his eyebrows and gave a thumbs-up. Others got a sturdy thumbs-down, and these he threw out of the closet to be donated to the clothing pool. Tinderella raised her own eyebrows in mild shock at the growing pile of clothes getting flipped out onto the floor.

She went to the lounge room to put some music on and decided on George Ezra and his latest album. She grabbed the bottle of bubbles and walked back into her room. Looking around, she couldn't see where Sam had gotten to.

'Sam?' she called out.

Sam swept out of the ensuite and into the bedroom like a diva—dressed in Tinderella's clothes. Her red sequinned dress, and her shiny red patent leather Manolo Blahniks. Her pride and joy! The sight of Sam in her dress hadn't really sunk in; it was the shock of seeing someone else in her beloved shoes that was causing her to go into a panic attack! Please be careful and please DO NOT scratch or mark them! she thought to herself.

Sam was in heaven. He proceeded out the bedroom door to the kitchen where his precious box had been waiting, holding the oversized dress close to his body so he could walk. He pulled on his white cotton gloves, opened it, and placed the priceless wrap around his shoulders.

Tinderella couldn't speak. She was aware she was staring but she couldn't help it, and she couldn't look away.

It was clear whom the wrap had been purchased for—and the penny dropped. Sam liked to wear women's clothing! She would never have guessed! She watched him prance around the lounge room, looking like the belle of the ball. Who was she to steal this moment from him? She raised her glass to Sam and started to cheer him on. If anyone had witnessed this scene, they would think the both of them were both nuts!

The phone rang. It was Sarah on the other end of the line, checking on her friend.

'Oh Sarah, you have to see this. Come over, quickly!'

Sarah arrived and entered the house to see a peacock in the making. Sam was in his element; he loved the audience.

Well, this date wasn't going to go any further, Tinderella thought, but what a joy it was to meet Sam and see him in his own natural light. She enticed him to take off the precious shoes, and to sit with her and Sarah so they could see the wrap and how delicate it was.

He obliged, stepping out of the heels in a very careful way, like an expert, and handed them to Tinderella with his gloved hands.

'I was looking after them, lovie,' Sam said in a cheeky voice.

Tinderella was relieved. No marks, no scratches. She guided Sarah into the kitchen, and they spoke in whispers as he went and redressed in his normal clothes.

'What is going on?' she asked Sarah, whose expression mirrored Tinderella's disbelief.

Who was this man who had come into her house and then outed himself as a cross dresser? Tinderella was more than fine with the whole scene but why was Sam on a dating site? And how often had he done this?

The time had come for Sam to go.

He gave Tinderella a passionate hug and Sarah a kiss on her hand. He was very likeable, in a cheeky, charming way. He picked up his precious box, with the exquisite wrap back in its original packing paper and handed it to Tinderella.

She was dumbstruck.

'Sweetie,' Sam said, 'this was always for you. Enjoy it and think of me every time you choose to wear it. Bon soir, my dear friends. We shall meet again one day!'

And with that, Sam was gone, leaving Tinderella and Sarah with a story to tell their friends.

But would their friends ever believe them?

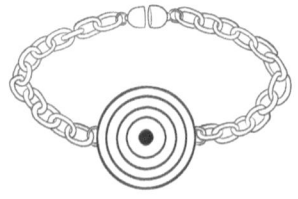

It's Time to Talk... by Simone

DATING IS A JOURNEY OF (SELF) DISCOVERY

You may not have expected to learn as much about yourself through dating as about the men you meet. But dating can truly open up your world, and with the right attitude, you will often gain more than just a new life partner at the end of your journey.

It's certainly not common for men to have a love of designer shoes and chick-flicks unless they're working in the fashion industry. How wonderful for Tinderella to find such a guy online. Through interacting with someone who shared her passion, Tinderella not only learnt more about Sam, she also gained greater knowledge about one of her favourite things.

The secrets we keep about ourselves

By the time we're adults, most of us have a skeleton or two in the closet—a secret source of guilt or shame which, if it were exposed, could wreck us, and which we therefore do our best to keep hidden. These 'skeletons' could be experiences from our past we're ashamed of, or something about our life right now we don't want made public. Despite Tinderella's experience, you're far more likely to meet a man who has 'come out of the closet' as gay than to have him literally come out of your closet wearing women's clothes.

A hint of what was to come was possibly evident in the ease with which Sam was able to switch between his two very different personas—high-profile newspaper editor in public, creative, passionate devotee of women's fashion in private. The care Sam took with his personal grooming and appearance when he met Tinderella indicates his interest included men's fashion, too.

It's refreshing to find a man who has a passion outside of and beyond his work, particularly when the two seem to be poles apart. This makes for wide-ranging conversations with depth and breadth.

AN INTRODUCTION TO CROSS-DRESSING

There is a growing awareness and acceptance of the full spectrum of human gender identity and sexuality—from gays, lesbians and bi-sexuals to transvestite, transgender and gender fluid individuals. Cross-dressing, by comparison, is still not widely understood or accepted, but it is more common than you might think. We're just not talking about it because there is stigma associated with it, and as a result men who cross-dress usually keep this fact intensely private for fear of judgement or ridicule. It's evident Sam was a confident and self-assured man to be so comfortable talking about fashion with Tinderella—let alone trying on her clothes in her home.

Men who cross-dress are not alone. There are dozens of online sites around the world that specialise in selling women's clothes, shoes and wigs to cross-dressers and transgender men. Many of these sites will also custom-make outfits for men to account for their different body shapes and can provide fashion advice on how to best bring out the 'woman within'. There are also hundreds of blogs, YouTube channels and Instagram accounts for men to explore their love of cross-dressing.

Why do men cross-dress?

Put simply, it's because they enjoy it, and for most, it is a strong need, far beyond a passing whim or fad. Men who cross-dress say they love wearing women's clothes and even wearing fake boobs because it gives them a deeply satisfying sense of freedom and self-expression. Some men are sexually aroused when they cross-dress but not all. Most men who cross-dress have no desire to become a woman and, in fact, consider themselves to be quite masculine. It's just that, in private, they like to release their inner woman.

Cross-dressing doesn't mean a man is gay or wants to have sex with men. Most male cross-dressers are sexually attracted to women and are in committed, loving relationships with a woman. Many of these men do keep their special interest a closely guarded secret, out of fear of how their partners will react. And it is a need — a compulsion — not just a passing desire.

Tinderella's experiences have shown us the distress caused by men on online dating sites who don't disclose elements of their life that could deter a woman from wanting a relationship with them. So, what a joy to see a man comfortably display and share his love of cross-dressing with a woman during their very first meeting. Yes, Sam and Tinderella had developed a connection through online messaging, and it's true he hadn't mentioned his love of cross-dressing—just his love of women's fashion—but how lovely that he sensed Tinderella would not be too shocked by him revealing his private self. It certainly made for a wonderful and memorable evening.

DATING ALLOWS US TO EXPLORE WHO WE WANT TO BE

Dating is a great way for people to explore not only what they are looking for in a partner, but also how they want to 'be' in a relationship. Women who find themselves single after many years in a relationship often realise they have been playing various roles in their former lives, such as wife/partner/mother/soccer mum/mum's taxi/cook/cleaner/career woman. But they have not always had the chance to be 'themselves'. Once they become single, many women feel adrift, and find they don't know 'what they want' in life, or in a partner.

Dating different guys provides you with opportunities to explore new interests and fun adventures such as places they like to visit or hobbies they enjoy. Online dating can be a fabulous way to explore what gives you joy in a way that puts you firmly in the driver's seat. Sam is clearly exploring what gives him joy. Perhaps his cross-dressing was not accepted by his previous partner and so he is online to find a woman who will accept him and love him regardless of his need to cross-dress. Or he may just be wanting to meet people like Tinderella who share his love of fashion.

One of the most delightful aspects to Sam's manner was his acceptance of his perceived shortcomings. His confident approach to his short stature was evident in his cheerful comment that 'good things come in small packages'. It's a refreshing quality to embrace yourself for who you are and how you look and is part of the work that allows happiness to come from within.

LEARNINGS FROM TINDERELLA AND SAM:

1. Not everyone on the online dating scene is looking for marriage. Some are looking for a connection with others who accept them for who they are.

2. Dating is a journey of self-discovery and provides the opportunity for people to explore who they want to be and what they want out of life.

3. Everyone has skeletons in their closet, and men who like to cross-dress generally prefer to keep this passion firmly in the closet, too. Cross-dressing is not necessarily a sexual fetish, nor an indicator a guy is secretly gay. Rather it is a behaviour or habit that can be accepted as a part of a man's personality and should not deter a woman from loving the person as a whole. Have fun with it and embrace it!

Chapter 15

Lenny

Self-righteousness has killed more people than smoking.

- John McCarthy

Lenny was dashing, in a Batman kind of way. He had dimples that were a danger to any girl. He reached out to Tinderella at a time when she had decided to let herself have a breather from the online dating minefield. He was an enthusiastic dater, 'all in' from the start, and wanted to see her the minute they started messaging each other on the dating site.

Tinderella was a little apprehensive. Her past experiences had left her feeling a little guarded, and she had started to lose interest in the whole scene. It felt as if she wasn't getting any return despite everything she'd invested in finding someone. She had just about put it in the too-hard basket.

She had started smoking again, too. She wasn't thrilled about it, but it was what it was. She knew she could quit in a matter of weeks, but in the meantime, she was a puffer. She'd tried the vapor, but it tasted worse and didn't do much. In the past she'd used the nicotine gums to quit. She believed the residual hurts of past relationships had made her create a crutch for herself. Smoking was the choice. She could feel the negative affects smoking had on her physical body, but fuck it! She would join the gym one day, but only when her lungs could breathe.

She had really embraced her 'I don't give a fuck' phase. She had succumbed to not having a shower before a date. She'd even stopped shaving her legs, anticipating the drought in her dating world. Living the dream, as they say.

In this frame of mind, she'd even thought about crossing over to date women, but sadly, it wasn't that easy. She was open-minded enough to consider the possibility, of course. If she ever did end up lusting after a chickie, and the feelings were mutual, maybe then it would happen. But this was just speculation. Tinderella knew she wasn't bisexual. She loved a man's masculine body and enjoyed it. She just had to put up with idiots and dickheads along the way. Maybe this was the way the Universe was finding the right guy for her? She imagined herself in combat gear, with a large hockey stick, whacking the toads out of the way. Hmmm ... that would be better, and faster. She smiled at the thought.

There was no denying her enthusiasm for dating had dwindled. The whole process had lost its sparkle. She was just going through the motions and it would take a lot of persuasion to leave behind the latest season of Game of Thrones. But Lenny was persistent, and Tinderella finally agreed to date him. One date only, just a quick drink at a local bar. It was walking distance from her home, so she could leave at a minute's notice. This guy had better be worth it, she thought.

They arranged to meet at 7pm. Tinderella had interstate friends visiting, and they had virtually taken over her whole house. There was no way she could bring Lenny back to her place, so that was good—a drink and they would part ways.

She had chosen to wear pants, because her leg hairs had grown so much she could now feel them moving in the wind. Her Brazilian had grown out into an Amazon, full and bushy—and she truly didn't give a crap. She had thrown on a long-sleeved silk shirt made more for comfort than sex appeal, and her loyal waterhole bracelet dangled from her left wrist. Her casual outfit suited her mood.

Since she was going through her protest phase, she even went so far to order herself a pint of beer. Every now and again, Tinderella liked a beer. It was refreshing and she could drink it down faster than a wine or cocktail. It helped pep up her mood when she was going through these moments. Her star sign reflected this. She was a moody person, and if someone pushed her buttons, she was more than capable of telling them—or the world—to fuck off.

And she was feeling pretty close to that now. Her online account had been hacked and she was being trolled by a guy she had never met before, talking crap about dating. His attacks were making her internal thermometer heat up, and she knew having a beer was a good thing for her. She would calm down, and get a little giggly and relaxed, and be able to disconnect from the troll and his comments. She had built a resilience through reading a book written by her friend and journalist, Ginger Gorman: *Troll Hunting*. It had helped ground her and understand trolls are bitter within themselves and she had nothing to blame herself for.

It was 7.18pm. Lenny was late. Just as Tinderella reached for her phone to check her messages, in he bounced. He apologised for his lateness and asked her if she wanted another drink.

No, Tinderella was fine.

She still had a third of her beer to drink, so he accepted her response. Lenny ordered himself a drink and also secured a menu, which impressed Tinderella.

'Would you like some food?' he asked, his dimples teasing her.

He was better looking in real life than he was in his profile photos. Secretly, she was glad she had agreed to meet up with him. Maybe she should have shaved her legs after all?

Nope! Tinderella, you need to refrain, and get to know this guy, she thought.

Lenny had a cheeky disposition. His conversation was easy and playful, and he made little jokes about his woeful dating experiences and the disappointments he had endured along the way. Tinderella found they seemed to share the same sense of humour, and Lenny was taller than her. That was definitely a plus in her book. For a night she had expected to be a chore, things were looking up! She was beginning to enjoy herself.

It was almost 9pm, and they hadn't even ordered anything to eat yet. They were completely caught up with getting to know everything possible about each other. The conversation was stimulating Tinderella's senses. She was actually having fun with this guy. So, they ordered dinner, and the conversation kept on flowing. Lenny offered to cover the cost of their meal, saying he was very pleased she had finally agreed to meet him so quickly—and, he'd been late, remember? The evening was going so well.

Tinderella asked Lenny if she could be excused and left him sitting at the table. She really needed to go out for a cigarette and hoped it wouldn't become a topic of discussion.

Outside in the warm summer night, she looked up at the dark sky. The bright stars looked closer tonight for some reason. She found herself so deep in thought she didn't notice Lenny had come out to get her. He tapped her elbow and startled her back to reality. Instantly, she felt guilty.

'I'm in the middle of quitting,' she told Lenny.

His mouth curved on one side, and he responded with: 'You will when you are ready.'

Hmm... he seemed very understanding. Not that she needed his approval, but she wasn't clueless. She knew it was bad for her body. She binned her butt and Lenny held the door open for her as she walked back into the bar. She reached into her purse and found her mints. She took two. Why am I so guilt-ridden about this? she asked herself. Maybe it was time to quit again.

Lenny pulled her chair out for her to sit. How charming!

The meals had arrived. They had been prepared with obvious creativity and expertise and they smelled delicious! They'd headhunted the chef from an acclaimed restaurant in the city in a bid to develop the dining experience at the bar and create a new vibe. It was working for Tinderella; she was impressed before even taking a mouthful.

Oh, wait!

'Let's take a photo of our meals and Instagram them,' Tinderella said. Lenny agreed, and this gave Tinderella a chance to lean over him and take a photo of his meal. The curve of her buttock rubbed against his arm and chest. Her forwardness amused Lenny and he held her hips still during the photographic moment.

Dinner tasted as good as it looked. Lenny offered Tinderella a bite of his sirloin steak. It literally melted in her mouth, and noises came from her throat that were a little too suggestive. Suddenly, she was Meg Ryan in the famous orgasm scene from *When Harry Met Sally*. They laughed together at her performance. Tinderella was relaxed and, for the first time in more dates than she could remember, had stopped checking the time on her phone.

Lenny asked Tinderella if she would like to go for a drive to another venue.

Decision time.

She agreed. He was a gentleman and opened the car door for her and made sure she was in the vehicle before closing it. He went around to the driver's side and got in, then leant over and looked her in the eyes. It was obvious he was going to kiss her and Tinderella was ready. She leant in and they kissed. It was a slow, soft, delicate kiss. It was a great first kiss, and it aroused her—she wanted more. She held onto Lenny's head and kissed him with a passion she hadn't felt in a very long time. It was wonderful to feel that way again, and he returned the kiss with equal fervour.

His hands found their way to her breasts, and he pulled at her nipples through her top. He started to unbutton her blouse and his right hand slipped into her bra to touch her bare nipple. The moment seemed to last forever. Tinderella praised the Universe for bringing Lenny into her world. He was worth the investment of going out on this date.

Lenny asked her to lower her car seat back. She found the correct button and reclined her seat. His hand travelled down her thigh and between her legs. He started to rub her there with the palm of his hand. Tinderella was feeling more and more turned on with every move. He slipped his hand into her pants; his fingers gently opened her slit, and he rubbed her clit in gentle, circular motions. It was responding, becoming erect with pleasure.

Lenny knew she was ready to have him inside her, and he whispered into her ear: 'Could I make love to you?'

Tinderella nodded, lost in a haze of passion. She had no words. There was an attraction between them. Would it last beyond tonight? Who knew? Right now, she wanted to feel like a woman again. She wanted to enjoy her body and allow a man to enjoy it too.

Lenny went around to her side of the car, raised her seat back up and made sure she was comfortable. He returned to his seat and started the car.

'Where should we go?' he asked her.

Her place wasn't possible—she had visitors. How about his place?

Lenny was renovating and staying with friends in a group house.

'Maybe if we drive somewhere, we can find a spot?' Tinderella suggested.

They started to drive. Lenny kept his hand between Tinderella's legs, stimulating her and keeping the mood alive. Finally, they found a quiet country road that led into a small town, just out of the city. If they could pull over somewhere and find a quiet spot, they could make love under the stars. They found an old, secluded church and Lenny pointed to the back of the building.

'That looks very private; let's go there,' he suggested.

Tinderella didn't mind where it was. She just wanted to ride this feeling to the end.

Lenny parked the car at the edge of the church's dirt carpark, under the trees, to provide a bit of camouflage for it. The last thing they needed was for visitors to come say hello during their moments of passion. He grabbed a large blanket out of the boot, then opened Tinderella's door for her.

'Follow me, gorgeous,' he said.

They held hands as they walked, crouching low so they couldn't be seen. Tinderella felt like a naughty schoolgirl who was going to end up in hell! Lenny spread out the blanket and sat down. Turning towards her, he held out his hand for hers, then pulled her down onto the blanket.

Tinderella was ready for him to have his wicked way with her. Soon there were arms and legs everywhere and Lenny was making sounds she had never heard a man make. Loud groaning noises—she worried he was going to attract attention! But Lenny wasn't going to be quiet any time soon. He was in the middle of lustful and passionate lovemaking, and Tinderella had to just let it go and not worry about the noise. So she began to make noises of her own! He pulled himself on top of her and began thrusting, pumping his manhood into her like a man on a mission. Tinderella liked it rough at times and this was taking her to a place of complete enjoyment. It felt fucking amazing, and they came together. It was a beautiful experience to feel a man reach climax at the same time as her.

Tinderella was satisfied. The night had turned out well after all.

But Lenny wasn't finished. He was still making love to her and was ready to go again. She was a more than willing participant. With a good lover, she could climax several times. He set her on top of him, holding her and moving her up and down whilst he watched her breasts bounce in the moonlight. Together, they came again.

Lenny lay Tinderella down in a way that let him put his face near her pussy. He was in awe of her bushy mound, and he stroked it lovingly, looking at it with desire in his eyes. His fingers opened her up, and he began to use his tongue to play with her. He had a gifted tongue, and it brought Tinderella to orgasm again. This time it was beyond anything she had previously experienced. It was like a tsunami, and Tinderella screamed with delight, relief and pleasure.

At this point, she was literally fucked by Lenny, and spellbound by him. He was a very good lover, and Tinderella hoped she would see him again in the future. They lay quietly together for a while under the stars, and then gathered the blanket and headed back to the car.

Lenny drove Tinderella home, all the while touching her leg and rubbing her knee. They kissed goodbye and Tinderella thanked him for such a beautiful night.

'Would you like to have another date?' she asked, feeling daring.

Lenny leant back and looked at her with puzzled amazement.

'Oh, no. Thank you, though. I could never seriously date a smoker. I'm happy to fuck you, but I will never have a relationship with you. Sorry.'

Ouch!

Another one bites the dust.

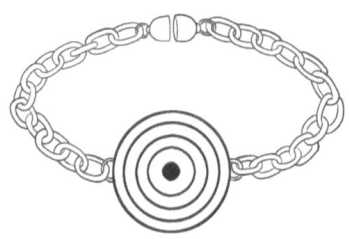

It's Time to Talk... **by Simone**

INTEGRITY—OR THE LACK OF IT—AND THE DATING SCENE

Which part of Tinderella's story did you find most concerning? That Lenny used her for sex, or dumped her for being a smoker? Although Tinderella's night initially seemed to offer much more than she had expected, this date is another example of a guy being dishonest about his intentions. Lenny knew he wouldn't date a woman who smokes, but he kept up the illusion there was indeed an attraction worth pursuing, purely for his own sexual needs. Perhaps even worse, Lenny made the decision for both of them that they weren't going to see each other again, because she was a smoker—regardless of whether Tinderella was planning to quit. Either way, he thought only of himself and his own needs, and he lacked the integrity to honestly state his intentions. It seems Tinderella dodged yet another bullet!

At the end of the day, he missed out on getting to know an amazing woman who has so much more to offer than just being defined as a smoker—so it's his loss. When it comes to the online dating scene, there is a lot of scope for dishonesty. Remember to do your due diligence, and practise dating safety basics.

DEALING WITH SMOKING AND RELATIONSHIPS

Smoking relates to health and lifestyle and should be something you consider when drawing up your *K.I.S.S. List for Mr Right*. For non-smokers, smoking in a partner can be a deal-breaker. They may find the smell offensive, even stomach-churning. Or they may be into fitness and view smokers as not valuing their own health and fitness—or their partner's (through issues such as second-hand smoke). Others of us are able to see past a potential new partner's smoking habit to their other endearing qualities.

There are a few things to consider before jumping into a relationship with someone whose attitude towards smoking is different to yours.

When you are the smoker

Your man could very well embrace the fact you smoke and never say anything discouraging about your smoking habit. Perhaps you and he have already discussed how to accommodate his needs regarding your smoking habit, such as making sure you smoke outdoors. However, the odds are you will at some point be lovingly encouraged to quit, because your non-smoking boyfriend will always be acutely aware of the dangers of smoking and will want you to be healthy and enjoy a long life with him. That loving encouragement could easily turn into nagging: 'Don't smoke there'; 'Don't have a smoke now'; 'Didn't you just have one?'; 'Do you know how much your habit is costing?'; 'Don't you want to grow old together?' No matter how kindly meant, we don't usually respond well to nagging, yet this is something you are highly likely to have to deal with.

When you are the non-smoker

You may begin with every intention of never nagging him or wanting to change him. Be aware over time, aspects of his smoking habit will likely become more and more annoying to you—the pervasive smell; the expense of his smoking habit; his smoker's cough; having to stop every couple of hours on a road trip or even the inability to take a long plane trip to a romantic destination; the anti-social aspect of smoking such as the impact of second-hand smoke on others (particularly children), disappearing regularly to smoke, and so on. A smoker's habit has a very high impact on those around them. Make sure you understand and accept what you are signing up for, because smoking can be a very hard habit to quit.

Why is smoking bad for you?

Tinderella could feel the effect smoking was having on her lungs, and she knew it wasn't good for her health. We know smoking cigarettes significantly increases your risk of developing cancer, for example. Tobacco companies have been forced to acknowledge this too. A 2006 judicial ruling in a lawsuit filed by the US federal government found that cigarette makers deliberately misled the public about the dangers of smoking[14].

Today's crisp, sterile-looking cigarettes are designed to look civilised and harmless, but they contain so many bitter-tasting chemicals the tobacco companies need to load them up with sugar to improve the 'taste'. Yes, cigarettes have sugar in them—a lot of it! That's another reason they are so addictive. Additives such as sugar and honey might seem harmless, but when the additives in cigarettes are burnt, they change into different chemicals, and some of these are toxic. For example, liquorice and sugar produce cancer-causing chemicals when burnt[15].

Why do people find it hard to quit?

Tinderella had tried different ways to quit previously and knew she would no doubt try again. Many people find it difficult to quit, and it can take a few attempts to finally manage it. This is because a smoker isn't just quitting the act of smoking. They must 'disconnect' all the emotional, physical and environmental triggers and associations connected with their smoking habit, as well as dealing with the physical symptoms of withdrawal. Routine and social interactions often drive a smoker's habit. For example, people tend to have a cigarette with coffee, drinks, and food; after sex; after arriving at a destination; before a meeting; before or after seeing a movie. Or they smoke because it's a certain time of the day, or they want a break from work, or a 'time out' from a person or situation.

Another reason why people find it hard to quit is because of what is happening on a subconscious level. Your subconscious mind makes up 90% of your mind's power and is programmed to 'draw you' to-

---

[14] https://www.npr.org/sections/health-shots/2017/11/27/566014966/in-ads-tobacco-companies-admit-they-made-cigarettes-more-addictive (a link to download the judicial ruling is included in this article).
[15] Talhout Rl, Opperhuizen A, van Amsterdam JG. https://www.ncbi.nlm.nih.gov/pubmed/16904804

wards the things that make you feel good—whether these things are good for you. So that leaves 10% of your mind (the part that wants to quit) to over-ride the other 90% of your mind's programming. As a result, conscious will-power (the 10%), isn't always enough to help people quit such an ingrained habit. Fortunately, there are other ways to help you quit than relying on your finite willpower alone.

How to quit smoking

My father died at the age of 47 from smoking-related cancer. This was devastating to our family as my dad was one of the most amazing, kind and gentle men you'd ever met. He tried so many ways to quit smoking before he died, but nothing worked for him. I made it one of my goals in life to develop a program that would help people successfully quit smoking. My Habit Breakers Quit Smoking Program uses hypnosis and neuro-linguistic-programming to help break the smoking habit at the subconscious level—where the habit is formed and stored. The program is now used successfully by psychologists, naturopaths and hypnotherapists to help their clients quit smoking.

There are also patches, gums and medications that work on a bio-chemical level to help your body reduce physical cravings for a cigarette. Plus, organisations such as Quit.org in Australia provide free online and telephone support for people trying to quit. The key is to find what works for you.

LEARNINGS FROM TINDERELLA AND LENNY:

1. It's your choice to smoke, or not to smoke. It's also your choice to date a guy who smokes, or not.

2. If you date someone who has different views to you on smoking, be prepared for what you're entering into. This can be a relationship deal breaker, so be upfront in your profile about your preferences as this is a factor that can potentially cause friction, especially if you are looking for a long-term relationship.

3. If you decide you want to quit smoking, there are plenty of ways to quit. Your body will definitely thank you for it, and it could open up more potential matches for you in your dating journey.

Chapter 16

Andrew

Why does the lizard stick his tongue out? Because that is its means of appreciating what's in front of it.

- William Shatner

'Tinderella has broken the Internet' will be on my gravestone, she thought to herself.

Every guy she saw online was someone she had dated, didn't find attractive enough to date, or was older than her neighbour's cat, which was at least one hundred years old in cat years.

And so, the two scariest words were heard: 'set up'.

She'd agreed to be set up on a date. The upside was that her close and trusted friends had arranged it. Surely they would be kind to her?

Apparently, Andrew was amazing. His wife had had an affair with her boss, and afterwards he had tried the online dating scene but had walked away from it unsatisfied. He had trust issues. Andrew had his guard up against women—his wife had betrayed him, and his ego wouldn't admit his loneliness. Her friends had plenty to say, sugar-coating things to lure her into the blind date.

'You'll be perfect for each other.'

'You will have an amazing future.'

'He's the best entertainer.'

Tinderella sat on her couch thinking about this dilemma, eating her favourite Hokey Pokey ice-cream. What was the worst that could happen? I could just have him over for a couple of drinks… we have mutual friends, so surely he wouldn't be crazy? She decided it was worth a try. She would date Andrew and her friends could play matchmaker. But no promises as to its success, she warned them.

Tinderella's phone rang moments later. It was Andrew. The conversation seemed to flow, with both of them laughing at the thought of their mutual friends scheming to get the two of them together. He was easy to chat to, and he asked Tinderella how she knew the couple who had introduced them. The conversation bounced from one subject to the other until it was time to work out a date night that would suit them both. They agreed on dinner at Tinderella's place in two days' time.

She wanted to impress Andrew, so she thought carefully about the presentation of her home and the menu. She decided to order in Yum Cha from a local restaurant. It would be quick and easy, sparing her hours in the kitchen. She could order a few different dishes, and plate them up at home. She tidied up a little and bought some flowers. Flowers always made the atmosphere a little happier.

Next thing to consider was what to wear?

Tinderella decided to go with something she already had in her closet, rather than buying a new outfit. She settled on a soft pink, loose-fitting one-shouldered top she had purchased from an upmarket department store. She hadn't worn it in a while, and it seemed the perfect choice for this occasion. A pair of three-quarter length skinny jeans and her favourite red shoes added to the outfit. Her hair was tied loosely up in a messy bun, and soft pieces fell down to frame her face in a romantic look. Her waterhole bracelet added the perfect finishing touch. It was still her favourite piece of Australian jewellery and helped keep her grounded. She secured the beautiful silver handmade piece on her left wrist. She was ready.

Tinderella stepped back to appreciate the finished result of her efforts. Everything looked great; the lighting was perfect, with the lights dimmed slightly, the house smelled inviting and the atmosphere was warm. The doorbell chimed. It was time for her to meet Andrew.

She opened her door, peeping round the edge of it, mentally cursing her friends in the process. Andrew was standing on her doorstep with a bright and cheery bunch of flowers, much like his smile, and he wasn't all that bad looking either, she decided.

She accepted the flowers and invited Andrew in. They exchanged a quick kiss on the cheek as he walked through the door. He then waited just inside the door, allowing Tinderella to take the lead. He hadn't been at her house before, and Tinderella was impressed he was being so charming.

She led him into the lounge room, where she had a bottle of pinot grigio chilling in a bucket of ice and two wine glasses sitting next to it, waiting for them.

Andrew took the cue and poured the drinks for them after looking to Tinderella to see if it was okay to do so.

She was pleased to see him take the lead. It was something she hadn't experienced in a while, and it was nice to sit back and soak up his attention. She instantly felt very relaxed with him, he seemed to be a pleasant guy to be around. He had a calming influence on her. It was an authentic, positive vibe, which also appealed to her in a life partner.

After taking the flowers to the kitchen, Tinderella offered Andrew a seat on the couch, and she sat with him and began to get to know him. She asked general questions about his hobbies and interests and what he did for work. It seemed they did have a fair bit in common, which was nice. It gave them a chance to share their own perspectives on life, love and living.

Tinderella found she was really enjoying his company and was glad she had arranged such a wonderful casual dinner. They decided to have their meal in the lounge room to keep with the relaxed feel. This man pleasantly intrigued her.

Andrew was a lawyer who had specialised in international law. He had always been passionate about travel and had created a very comfortable lifestyle for himself where he was paid to travel, consulting with his extensive list of international business law clients. He seemed to have it all together and Tinderella was impressed.

So why then was a guy like this single?

Tinderella put this question to Andrew.

He explained his job was almost like a marriage and required a high percentage of his time and energy. He could be asked to fly to an international location at a moment's notice. For many women, his working away proved to be a challenge, but he reassured Tinderella there would be potential travel for his future partner, too, if the opportunity presented itself. He also explained his ex-wife had felt the loneliness of this and had chosen to go outside their marriage for companionship. A fact that had hurt him deeply.

The idea of travel appealed to Tinderella. Her love for cultures from around the world could be seen by the artefacts on display in her loungeroom. They were cherished reminders of her many overseas holidays experiences. Mind you, she hadn't been to Europe or America yet. She had done a few smaller trips, but there were many more on her bucket list.

Tinderella wanted to see London, Rome, and climb the Eiffel Tower in Paris. She dreamed of kissing her beloved in the heart of that romantic city, followed by a seductive night in a Parisian hotel suite. This would be a dream come true for her. Travel was one very exciting part of the future she dreamed of for herself.

Andrew was talking very softly now, looking deep into her eyes. He had just the right amount of confidence and charisma. A natural leader, Tinderella thought. Another tick of the box on her 'K.I.S.S. List for Mr Right'. He could feel the positive energy and with this, he leant in to kiss Tinderella on her beautiful full mouth. She could feel her heart beating inside her chest as she accepted his mouth on hers.

Andrew's hands found their way to cradle Tinderella's face, and he kissed her deeply.

Tinderella nearly gagged.

His kissing technique could only be likened to horror stories. His long tongue had not only penetrated the inside of her mouth, it had reached down to the back of her throat. It was repulsive.

He finished his tongue dive and leant back to look at her intensely.

'Almost like deep throating, hey?' he asked her.

Tinderella was in shock; this couldn't be the same guy, surely?

Andrew took Tinderella's silence for approval and guided her to lie down on the couch. Within seconds he was on top of her and began to repeat the process. Tinderella was literally gob smacked!

What. The. Fuck?

His face was an inch or so away from hers and he looked at her. Andrew's lips pursed and he let spit come from his mouth onto her face.

OMG! Is this guy spitting on me?

Is this his fucking foreplay?

Tinderella was frozen for an instant as she processed what was happening.

Where the fuck did he learn this shit? she thought. In what millennium did he think this was appropriate? Finally coming back to reality, she managed to pull herself out from under Andrew and stand up.

She had had quite enough of Andrew. With a look of absolute fury, she extended her arm and pointed to the door, with a swift jerk to indicate the night was over. Andrew looked a bit sheepish and was lost for words. Tinderella stood her ground and indicated the door again. By this time, her fury had doubled, and she was ready to find something to throw at him.

Yes, Tinderella was fucking pissed.

The jerk! Andrew had crossed the line.

He slowly got up from the couch, watching Tinderella warily. He was virtually in a crouch position, ready to run. Tinderella reached for a cushion and threatened to whack him over the head with it.

Andrew took that as his cue to exit as fast as he could and, still speechless, he was out the door.

Urgh! Yuck! Tinderella rushed to her bathroom and washed her face with anti-bacterial face wash and brushed her teeth in a frenzy. She was gagging at the memory of what had just happened. Wiping her face dry, she picked up her phone and began to call her friends. They had better be ready for an earful, because Tinderella was ready to explode!

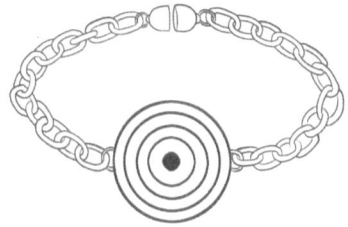

It's Time to Talk... by Simone

THE PITFALLS OF MATCHMAKING

Our friends always want the best for us. When those friends are in loving relationships, more than likely they naturally want that for us, too. So, when they come across a single guy who ticks all the boxes of the sort of partner *they* think would suit us, or even ticks all *their* boxes, they will gladly send them our way.

Despite the best of intentions, matchmaking by friends is not always a great idea.

Firstly, unless your friends know you very well and are privy to your *K.I.S.S. List for Mr Right*, what our friends see as a potential match for us may not be who we would consider to be a potential match.

Secondly, if it doesn't work out this can result in a little awkwardness between you and your friends. This may never go away, because friends can interpret the rejection of their male friend as a rejection of themselves.

Finally, if things do end badly between you and their male friend, it can be difficult for all parties if you are in their inner circle of friends as you may cross paths in the future and an obvious awkwardness may occur.

Leave it to the professionals

Professional matchmaking services provide a premium, personalised offering with your interests in mind. They will usually interview you to find out what you are looking for in a partner and will only refer possible matches to you that fit your profile specifications. The cost associated with this service is a lot more than what you pay for an online dating service.

If you decide to go down this route, do your homework first and find out the success statistics of the business. Look at the number and quality of the current 'pool' of single men they have on their books. It's also useful to know how they attract new clients.

Insider tip: type the business name and the word 'scam' into a search engine to reveal any disgruntled stories from previous unhappy clients.

AN INTRODUCTION TO KISSING

Not all men are princes, and you may need to kiss a few frogs along the way. Andrew's story highlights that physical looks and attraction are just one part of the chemistry that connects suitable partners. The way a guy kisses can be a telling indicator of compatibility.

The term 'great kisser' is a quality many people look for in a suitable mate. There's no right or wrong way of kissing. Everyone's kissing technique is different. Here are some types of kisses:

- Butterfly kisses—placing kisses lightly on your man's face
- Eskimo kisses—noses gently rubbing together
- Lip kiss and suck—taking your guy's lip into your mouth and gently sucking it
- Lizard kissing—using your tongue to kiss his tongue (note: tongue to tongue—not tongue to tonsils!)
- French kissing—exploring each other's inner mouth with your tongues
- Neck kissing—gentle kisses and sometimes gentle sucks on each other's necks

And of course, kisses aren't just meant for the lips or face. Exploring your partner's entire body with your lips and tongue is deeply erotic.

Ask for what you enjoy and don't tolerate anything less

Sometimes guys just need a little help with the art of kissing. A little gentle guidance and feedback goes a long way—just like showing a man what you love during sex and what he can do to help bring you to orgasm. If he is receptive and eager to please you, that says a lot about him, and his desire to pleasure you is likely to bring you even closer.

Andrew's use of his tongue in a probing, almost choking manner is likely more about dominance, and nothing at all about intimacy. He was using his tongue as an extension of his penis in an attempt—whether consciously or unconsciously—to exert his masculinity and gain control.

Spitting on Tinderella's face was also very odd, and highly offensive to her, as spitting on someone is a significant cultural offence in our society. His action was more than just sloppy, wet kissing that leaves the recipient feeling they've just been through a car wash. Saliva can be used on a woman's vagina to increase lubrication, so perhaps Andrew had totally mistaken Tinderella's mouth for her vagina! Whatever his reasons, it's highly unlikely this frog will find a princess.

LEARNINGS FROM TINDERELLA AND ANDREW:

1. Be cautious about the guys your friends introduce you to. It's likely you'll only be '6 degrees of separation' away from each other, if not within each other's inner friendship circles. If an introduction doesn't work out, make sure to thank your friends anyway, and stay polite in your communication with the guy to keep awkwardness to a minimum. Of course, if it does work out, you'll both be forever grateful to your friends for seeing the potential and taking that chance to introduce you!

2. If you'd prefer to take the guesswork and time-wasting out of dating, then a professional match-making service may be an option. It's more costly than online dating subscriptions, or the occasional free recommendations from trusted friends or family. It may be worth trying if you're short of time and are happy to pay for premium quality, personalised match-making assistance. As with all such endeavours, remember to do your due diligence.

3. Kissing is an important aspect of a loving relationship. It is an act of intimacy as much as an act of sexual arousal. There are many types of kisses and the way a guy kisses will make you want more or will turn you off him. Andrew's kiss was likely an act of masculine sexual dominance, rather than intimacy. If you don't like the way a guy kisses, you can tactfully try to teach him how you do like to be kissed. If you are completely revolted by his style or physical presence, then it's okay to move on to the next guy.

Chapter 17

Ron

"Odors have a power of persuasion stronger than that of words, appearances, emotions, or will...there is no remedy for it"

- Patrick Suskind, in
Perfume: The Story of a Murderer

It was a shame people knew Ron was about to enter a room long before he actually did.

Ron had the ability to alienate everyone around him without even trying. It wasn't that he had an irritating way about him, or he had a huge ego that couldn't be withstood. He was a pleasant man, a clean 6/10 on the dating scale. He wasn't what some would call ugly, or uncivilised, and he could chat about any number of things if he had the chance to speak, but he had a problem.

Tinderella was about to discover his Achilles heel.

Online, Ron was witty. She found him to be a great conversationalist, and one particular conversation revealed he was often the one asked on dates by women. He just couldn't seem to make it further than the first twenty minutes of every date, as his dates always seemed to have an emergency, or they had double-booked themselves or had some other reason to make a quick departure. Tinderella had started chatting online to him a few weeks back, and she thought he was a nice guy.

At the risk of sounding superficial, she'd started to wonder if she should lower her standards and her expectations about her dates. Who knew? Maybe an average Joe wasn't going to turn her on physically, but perhaps there would be a deeper connection...

Ron was such a guy, and he was Tinderella's date for the evening. Well, it was more of a 'linner'—not quite lunch, and not dinner, since it was a 3.00pm meet up. Tinderella giggled at the thought of her new word and wondered if it was in the dictionary.

She decided to downplay her appearance for this date, as she didn't want to scare Ron off with a glamourized version of herself. She knew she scrubbed up well and could look stunning with the right outfit and make-up, but not today. She would play the understudy role so as not to put too much pressure on Ron. If a second date was on the cards, she could dress as a knockout then.

Tinderella opted for her three-quarter length jeans with patches, a red one-shouldered top and her waterhole bracelet. Simple, easy and no need to think too hard. But she couldn't resist wearing her red stilettos. She loved red. Her nails were red, and they matched her lipstick. Tinderella was only sad she had yet to find a lipstick that stayed on and didn't leave red stains everywhere. Especially when it came to kissing.

What the heck, she thought. Please Universe, find me a red lippy that stays! Maybe she should manufacture one?

She smiled at her completed look. Who was she kidding? She looked hot, and she knew it!

Tinderella was running a few minutes late and messaged Ron to tell him she was two minutes away. Ron responded pleasantly and told her to take her time. She found a parking spot directly outside the café-bar they had agreed to meet at, which saved her a few minutes of walking time. She liked the venue. It was light, airy and casual, and the beer on tap was a favourite.

Tinderella walked inside, scoping the premises for Ron. She soon saw a man sitting on his own, whose face looked familiar to his profile picture, so she headed over. He looked up, and she noticed his eyes open wide with appreciation on her approach. He stood as she arrived at the table. Ron was clearly nervous.

Tinderella wasn't, so much. She had adopted a more laid-back approach to dating and learnt not to get her hopes up on the first date. She would stay detached. She had cried too many times before when her expectations had not been met. Times when her hopes were squashed like a bug on the windscreen of life. But not just any bug; a big fat one that squirted its guts out all over the glass. The kind that was a complete fucker to get off the windscreen without a paint scraper. Hence the detached approach. To be honest, she felt it gave her more control, as she wasn't getting as emotionally invested as she used to in the early days. It felt a little sad because it probably wasn't the most positive approach to meeting someone for the first time.

Well, it is what it is, she thought.

Ron leant forward to kiss her on the check, and Tinderella smiled. He was well-mannered and perhaps a touch awkward, but she reassured him, saying she was nervous too, and this seemed to relax him as his shoulders dropped a fraction.

Whilst standing there, Tinderella became aware there was an unusual smell in the venue today, almost like dead prawn shells left in the sun, and it stung Tinderella's nose slightly, but she chose to ignore it.

Tinderella decided that since he had waited, she would offer to buy the first drink. Ron replied he would have a lemon, lime and bitters, and Tinderella went to the bar.

There she became completely distracted by the gem of a guy mixing the drinks in front of her. He was a master at making cocktails, throwing the bottles around like they were playthings in the park. His biceps were bulging under his neat white shirt and Tinderella didn't mind waiting to be served. She watched him with a sexual craving that came from deep within her.

It wasn't long before he turned his attention towards her and flashed his sexy pearly-whites at her, asking what she needed. With a jolt, she was back in reality. She was on a date with Ron. But, oh my—the bartender was cute!

She paid for the drinks and took them back to where Ron was waiting. He looked very anxious, and she wondered if he had perhaps witnessed her body language toward the barman? He took the drink she offered and drank it like a thirsty camel. He was almost gulping it down, not allowing the straw to do its proper job. Tinderella sipped her beer and watched Ron in awe. He was certainly a puzzling man, a little quirky perhaps?

Oh, well. She sat and looked at Ron, ready to start the conversation.

Ron cleared his throat and started talking. Did his voice just crack with nervousness?

He was telling Tinderella about his work, and his past experiences with dating, when Tinderella noticed something awful. She looked around the table. There was no one was close by, but the odour had suddenly intensified. It was invading her nostrils and travelling to her lungs. It was so bad, so acidic, it made her want to dry-retch. The spew-worthy smell was nothing short of horrendous.

She couldn't possibly *not* say anything. It was like smelling hell itself.

'Ron,' Tinderella interrupted, 'can you smell that?'

He began to turn red. Not just any red. It was a dark, beetroot red that started on his neck and travelled to cover his whole face.

Tinderella had her hands to her own face. She couldn't stand the smell that was invading their table. She looked at Ron, who was, by then completely embarrassed.

Oh no, Tinderella thought. Did he just fart? He was showing all the signs of a guilty party. Ron had just dropped the worst fart Tinderella had experienced in her life! She could live another fifty years and never smell anything else as horrid come out of someone's butt!

Ron began to apologise. He was clearly desperately uncomfortable, and wore a look of shock on his face, indicating his bowels had betrayed him. He explained he had a bodily function he couldn't control. He had a bad gas problem.

Bad gas? What an understatement!

This was fuckity fuck fuck! It was too much! The smell hadn't yet left the table. It felt as though it had now penetrated her clothes!

Tinderella couldn't help it. She had to ask Ron exactly what the problem was.

Ron told her he had irritable bowel syndrome. Whenever he was anxious, nervous or stressed, his body would expel gas. By now, Tinderella felt physically ill and she couldn't sit for a minute longer. She excused herself to go to the bathroom and Ron just nodded sadly. She left her beer at the table; it was only a quarter down, but it was worth the exit. Sacrifice the beer for fresh air, she thought.

Tinderella couldn't remember being so pleased to breathe in the smell of a toilet before! She looked in the mirror, and yes, her face literally was green. Oh, how was she going to leave this date without hurting Ron's feelings? Maybe she could do a runner? She remembered their table was positioned very close to the door, with her car just outside, so that was impossible. How was she going to get out of this? Think, Tinderella, think....

She regained her composure a little and exited the bathroom. Suddenly, her feet wouldn't work. It was as if they were glued to the floor just outside the ladies' bathroom door. They didn't want to go back into the danger zone, and she couldn't blame them. She was stuck. Just at that moment, the sexy barman walked past and noticed her distressed state.

He asked her if she was okay, and Tinderella explained her situation. The look of fear in her eyes must have been convincing, because the barman led her out the back way, via the service entrance and opened the back door for her. Tinderella was so grateful and relieved. She embraced him in a big hug. It was totally reactive to the situation, and a little ballsy, she knew, but oh, he felt good. The barman felt the obvious relief in her body as she relaxed in his arms. He looked at her and leant in to kiss her. Tinderella, although a little shocked, accepted his mouth on hers; it was so passionate, yet soft and sweet.

'Don't worry, honey,' the barman told her. 'You're a hot chick. Head out the back door and find a better guy... or better still, here's my number. Maybe we can hook up sometime?'

Tinderella couldn't believe her luck and the way the Universe was working. It truly was amazing how things could change in a matter of a few minutes. Life was looking fabulous! She quickly exited the building and snuck to where her car was parked. She could see Ron was still sitting at the same table, waiting for her to return.

She felt a terrible sense of guilt, but there was just no way she could go back into the terrible fog surrounding her date. She sank down in her car seat as she pulled out of her parking spot, merged into the lane of traffic, and made her getaway.

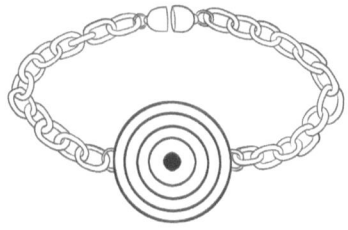

It's Time to Talk... by Simone

DEALING WITH DATING NERVES

Dating nerves can be brutal. At some point in our lives, most of us have will have experienced a nervous tummy when we're about to enter or actually in a situation we'd rather not suffer through.

The physical experience of 'nervousness' can include a racing heart, sweating, shaking, dry mouth, butterflies in the tummy, or tummy rumblings and nausea. These symptoms are usually caused by physical changes that occur in your body when your mind perceives a person you are with, or a situation you are about to enter, as 'dangerous' (whether real or imagined). Your body goes into what's called a stress response. A series of chemical and hormonal reactions, such as a rush of adrenaline, occur naturally in the body to prepare it for fight, flight or freeze to keep you safe from the perceived danger.

This is understandable when there's a real danger, but not so great when there is no actual peril. Our bodies will still interpret our thoughts, worry and anxiety as a sign of danger that must be prepared for. The resulting physical reactions caused by worry or nervousness can be quite debilitating—including the symptoms associated with Irritable Bowel Syndrome (IBS) and other gut issues. Unfortunately for some, a nervous tummy quickly leads to flatulence or even diarrhoea, typical symptoms of IBS. Others include abdominal pain, cramps, bloating and the sudden need to go the toilet.

It's estimated that 1 in 5 people have IBS to varying degrees and it is more common in women than men. So the chances are, you or your date can relate to this story. Some people are so affected by IBS they always need to know in advance where the closest toilets are, in case they have an urgent need to go to the loo. They can become quite anxious and almost phobic due to the fear they have of farting around others or soiling their pants. This anxiety in turn actually increases the likelihood of that happening.

Causes of IBS

IBS issues are centred on the gastrointestinal tract (the gut), and can be exacerbated by stress, worry, food intolerances and more.

Causes of IBS include:

- Problems with the mechanics of the gut—the intestinal muscles moving food through the tract become over or under-active, resulting in diarrhoea or constipation; and/or the nerves within the tract become oversensitive, resulting in pain.
- Infections in the gut—caused by bacteria, viruses or parasites.
- Genetics—you're more likely to have IBS if other members of your family also have it.

Other causes of flatulence

Flatulence such as what Ron has been experiencing is a known symptom of IBS, but this is not necessarily the only cause. Other causes of the embarrassing smelly fart or 'sharting' (shitting and farting at the same time!), include eating certain foods or drinks that are known to cause excess gas build-up in the stomach, such as beans, cauliflower and soft drinks. Flatulence is also caused by lactose and other food intolerances, and even by excessive swallowing of air.

What to do if you have a nervous tummy

There are certain things that can trigger an IBS 'attack' that can be avoided—particularly when going on a date. If you know you have a nervous tummy in certain situations, here are some suggestions to help prevent embarrassing situations such as Ron's:

- See your GP for diagnosis, treatment and management of your nervous tummy or gut issues and clarify whether you have any food intolerances. There are medications that can help reduce or even eliminate symptoms. Alternative treatment options are also available through naturopaths, chiropractors, hypnotherapists and more.

- Before your date, do some deep breathing relaxation exercises to calm your nervous system (making your body stand down from 'danger mode'). This also helps you to avoid sucking in too much air due to anxiety.
- Avoid milk products, i.e. lactose, in the lead up to and during your date. That includes cheese and ice cream!
- Avoid bubbly, fizzy drinks such as champagne or soft drinks in the lead up to and during your date.
- Avoid eating foods in the lead up to and during your date known to increase gas production in the gut, such as cabbage, beans and onions.

Ron must have known he had some gut issues, as it's highly likely he could smell his own stinky farts—just as Tinderella could. It's also likely he's aware his farts are the reason he is repelling people. So why hasn't he sought help for this problem? He may be so embarrassed about his condition he doesn't want to talk about it with anyone, even his GP. Or perhaps he doesn't realise there is help available to manage or even treat his condition. Regardless, it's neither realistic nor courteous to expect your date to simply ignore the assault on their olfactory system. It's also disrespectful to colleagues at work if this is happening on a regular basis with no remedial action taken.

We're all human. It's absolutely okay and normal to fart accidentally on occasion, no matter how much you 'hold it in'. It's one thing to feel sorry for Ron, but it's also difficult to explain away what could be better managed by him out of respect for those around him, and for his own health and wellbeing. Despite any embarrassment, if you focus on courtesy it's easy enough to excuse yourself if you've accidentally farted, or to go to the bathroom if you feel a fart or a funny tummy coming on. The fact Ron didn't do either shows disrespect for his date, regardless of any nerves or anxiety that may have exacerbated his gut issues.

It's therefore completely understandable that Tinderella would walk away, in this case straight into the arms of a gorgeous—and no doubt better-smelling—new man.

LEARNINGS FROM TINDERELLA AND RON:

1. It's not uncommon to feel nervous in certain situations, such as meeting a guy for the first time. It's also not uncommon for people to experience tummy problems in these situations. In fact, 1 in 5 people experience IBS symptoms to varying degrees, including involuntary farting or diarrhoea.

2. You can avoid known triggers of tummy problems, including dairy products, fizzy drinks and yeast products. If you have noticed a reaction to these foods, it may be worth exploring whether you have an intolerance. Some foods can actually help alleviate symptoms and improve gut health, and a change in diet can make a huge difference to gut issues. Treatment and symptom management support is available from GPs and dieticians as well as naturopaths, chiropractors and hypnotherapists.

3. If you accidentally fart, and it stinks or even just makes a loud noise, don't pretend it didn't happen. It's a normal bodily function. It's okay to apologise or turn it into a laugh—but at the very least own it if you can't escape it!

Chapter 18

Derrick

Astrology is like a game of chess with an invisible partner.

- Noel Tyl

Tinderella had messaged with Derrick over the past six months, just general chitchat, without anything too hot and heavy. At times, they would message each other for hours on end, and then there would be a digital silence that would last for days at a time.

This suited Tinderella. She wasn't overly invested in Derrick as she had been juggling two other guys online. Having learnt from her past date failures, she wasn't willing to focus on a single date until there was real potential to see it go further. This allowed her to take a more casual approach and avoid creating something in her own mind that didn't exist. Sometimes, over-thinking things made Tinderella her own worst enemy in dating. Her imagination and fear would overtake the positive in her head, her heart and sabotage her current existence.

She had promised herself she'd stop her fantasising and overthinking with Derrick, and true to her promise, she had kept it very casual so far, perhaps even a little too aloof. So it was surprising when he sent her a message asking to meet up. Tinderella thought he would be an interesting character to meet. He often dropped little scientific and astrological statements into his messages that Tinderella didn't quite understand, but often responded to with interest. Meeting him would allow her the opportunity to learn some more.

Derrick suggested they meet at the Arboretum and watch the sun go down over a glass of wine and nibbles. It was a beautiful spot on the edge of town with sweeping views across the city. Tinderella agreed, and he asked her to bring a blanket, and a chair if she wanted.

She thought she would opt for cushions, as an extra, as they would be much nicer to sit on, and easier to carry. He would be bringing the wine and a hamper of snacks to graze on during the sunset.

Tinderella was relieved the proposed outing would allow her to dress casually and relax. There was little time to put too much planning into her outfit, in fact, as Derrick had suggested they meet that night. It was something to do with the moon's position in the solstice, or the sky—she wasn't really sure of the particular reason. She chose a favourite comfortable and well-worn pair of dark blue denim jeans, matching them with a lovely beige poncho she had purchased online, and a pair of short light brown boots that complemented the outfit perfectly. For some reason, she had forgotten to take off her treasured waterhole bracelet in the last week. It still hung from her wrist. She removed it as she got ready for her spiritual bath and laid it next to her date clothes.

Tinderella turned on a little mood music and eased into the warm bath dosed with the salts she had purchased from her spiritual healer. She felt like a soak instead of a shower, and the salts promised to help bring love into her world. She could relax for a while and then shave her legs. They were well and truly overdue and looked like a winter hedge gone mad.

She sat in the warm water, reflecting on her many previous dates. She was puzzled as to why in so many meetings had she not found a good match. There was always a twist, or surprise, something that side-swiped her during each and every one of them. How was she meant to find the right one in this minefield of men? She knew the answer. She had to keep going. She simply wouldn't quit. He had to be out there somewhere, and she wasn't willing to stop looking for her soul mate just yet.

The weeks had turned into months since she had physically connected with anyone. She had been busy with her kids, her businesses and life in general. It was important to her that she keep her social life open and connected, especially contact with her soul sisters, her very special girlfriends. The last thing she wanted was to alienate her friends while trying to find Mr. Right.

Tinderella wondered if Derrick might be 'the one'.

She thought about herself as a person.

Was she doing something wrong?

Was she setting the bar too high?

Was her expectation that there was a right guy for her a total fantasy?

'Time will tell,' she whispered to her polished toenails peeking out of the top of the water. The bath water had cooled, and it was time to get out. Tinderella reached for her Egyptian cotton towel, which was her favourite colour—bright turquoise blue—stepped out of the bath and wrapped herself in luxury. There was no better way to end a spiritual bath, and she hoped the salts had done their magic.

She stood in front of the mirror and picked her body apart.

Oh, why do I do this to myself?

She hadn't been to the gym in years. It was a long time since she had put herself first. She had spent most of her life putting others first, and now she was single, she was exploring ways to become the person she was always meant to be. She knew she still had a long way to go, but every day was a new day. She intended to keep pushing herself out of her comfort zone to grow.

Today was one of those days!

So here she was, preparing for another date with a man she hardly knew. She was nervous, as with every new meeting, but the experience of being brave enough to meet with someone new aligned with her philosophy in life. It was a step toward her life goals and where she saw herself in her future.

Her dream was to have a life partner who enriched her in every way. Tinderella knew she was naturally a nurturer, a caregiver, and she needed to find a man who matched her soul. Someone who would spoil her in the way she desired. Her 'K.I.S.S. List for Mr Right'— which she'd kept updating throughout her experiences—described the type of a guy she wanted, and she needed the Universe to find him for her. Tinderella wanted a guy who could help keep her balanced and protect her. She needed someone who was a conversationalist and had his own passions and dreams. She needed her guy to have his own ambitions, and she wanted to support him through all of his life goals and desires, as he would hers. Tinderella had visions of her man being a nice height, where she could easily wear her stilettos and fit perfectly into his arms. Visually, Tinderella was an 'arms, chest and face' girl, and secretly, she needed him to have a good level of fitness, so they could enjoy experimenting with multiple sexual positions.

Still looking in the mirror, Tinderella promised herself to spend more time on her body. She would bring more peace and balance into her life, by putting herself first. This was an act of self-care, not selfishness. She had started meditating and visualizing, which was giving her a more positive approach to life.

Tinderella dressed for her date and applied her makeup in colours that would coordinate with her outfit. She had been to the nail salon the day before and her nails were painted a rich red colour. She sat on her bed to put her waterhole bracelet back on. She admired the design—the tunnel image reminded her of love. It was like the layers of an onion, and she needed to peel the layers back and find the one she desired.

The clock chimed five. It was time to meet her date. She picked up her car keys, and walked into her garage, admiring her beautiful white Mercedes Benz convertible. It was her dream car, and she had worked so hard to achieve this for herself. It had taken her over thirty years to realise this dream, and she'd put blood, sweat and tears into it. Two years ago, she'd dared to put a picture of this car on her vision board, where she could see it during the endless nights at her desk, working to see her businesses become sustainable. Finally, she'd hit her goal. She had actually cried when she was able to make the purchase, and now the keys were in her hand.

Tinderella followed the Law of Attraction and believed in the manifestation of everything in her life. She had created vision boards and hung motivational quotes around her house. This kept her focused and helped her to maintain her goals every day. Initially, she had started with small wins, and rewarded herself with small gifts. Like her new flashy kettle, the new Dyson vacuum cleaner, and her new stainless steel double door fridge. Finally, she had manifested her most amazing goal, her car, and she loved it fiercely.

Tinderella arrived at the Arboretum in record time. She collected her things, and an extra bottle of wine, and walked to the agreed meeting spot. She laid the blanket out on the grass, under a collective group of trees, with a good view to the sunset. She scattered the cushions on it and sat, waiting for Derrick to arrive.

Within a few minutes, a man approached her and introduced himself as Derrick. He was a lot shorter than she anticipated, but she wasn't going to let this influence their initial meeting. It was important she get to know him for the person he was.

He sat down on the blanket and unpacked the snacks and wine he had brought for them to enjoy. Tinderella was impressed he had put some thought into preparing for their time together—and he had remembered to include glasses for the wine! He filled their glasses while she opened the snacks and they began to talk about general things. Although there seemed to be a few areas in which they were not compatible, she had held off deciding whether he was the guy who had a future with her.

The sun was setting, and the sky was a multitude of warm colours. There were beautiful sparkling golds, and shimmering shades of reds, oranges and purples. Together, they watched the show taking place in front of them. Nature was amazing; it created pure magic every day. Some things are beyond words; they need to be experienced to be believed. This was one of those times. Tinderella couldn't find the words to explain the picturesque view in front of them at that very moment. Admittedly, it was very romantic, and she was feeling less nervous. As she'd driven herself there, she'd planned to have only one glass of wine. She was making it last, but it seemed this was an occasion that warranted more than one glass, so she was glad there was a local service called PKUP that could deliver her and her beloved Mercedes home safely when the time came.

Derrick started to talk about the sun and its position in the astrological galaxy. He spoke of its impact on the planets, the cycles, the moon and the earth. He was clearly obsessed with astronomy and astrology. This was a new level for Tinderella, way out of her usual league of reading her stars in the local magazine. If there was a good message, she went with it, but if it was a less than happy reading, she disregarded it. Other than that, she knew very little about astrology.

The sun had all but vanished, and it had become more of a sky show than a sunset. The hues painted across the horizon mesmerised Tinderella.

Derek pulled her back to reality with a single statement.

'I'm so happy that your star sign is Leo, as we could be very compatible in many ways—physically, emotionally. Tell me, do you feel a synchronicity with the pair of us?'

Tinderella was taken aback as she had never really discussed her star sign with Derrick, and she wondered how he had reached this conclusion.

'Derrick,' she said, 'I'm a little confused. While I'm not completely familiar with astronomy, I do know my star sign isn't Leo. My star sign is Cancer, the Crab.'

As she completed her sentence, she watched Derrick's face start to fall apart. He looked as though he had just tasted something that was completely vile, and his expression turned to horror.
She had never seen such a reaction to something that, to her, seemed so minor. Derrick looked as if he'd accidentally kissed a dog's bum and was ready to throw up.

Are you kidding me right now? she thought. Was this man so obsessed with finding his compatible star sign partner he could be so disrespectful?

'Oh, I am truly sorry, Tinderella,' Derrick apologised, 'but I must have you mixed up with another woman I'm talking to. I cannot possibly engage with a non-compatible star sign. I am sorry, dear, but you just aren't the one for me.'

As he spoke, he collected the items he had bought along to the picnic. Tinderella watched in disbelief. He stood and indicated he needed to go by looking at his Apple Watch as confirmation.

'Ah, I must head off,' he said absentmindedly. 'Um, thanks for the meeting. I—um, must head off. Ah, yes, I'll—um, be in touch,' he stammered.

With that, Derrick quickly turned on his heel and scuttled off as if he had ants in his pants. He couldn't have looked more desperate to leave. Tinderella looked for her glass. It had vanished, and she looked up in time to see Derrick tipping out her wine whilst making his quick getaway. Shocked, she watched him disappear into the distance.

'Oh, you have got to be kidding me. What a tosser!'

Fortunately, she had her own bottle of wine. She was going to sit on her blanket and take in the city lights. Since Derrick took the glasses, Tinderella picked up her bottle of wine, unscrewed the top and began drinking it from the neck.

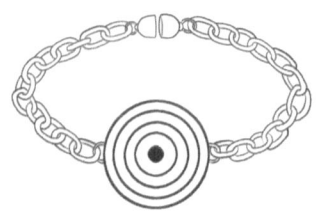

It's Time to Talk... by Simone

DEALING WITH DATING UPS AND DOWNS

It's perfectly natural to feel disheartened at times during your journey searching for your true love. Most of the time, dating is a great way to be reminded about all your good qualities and the things about you guys find attractive. Going on a date can be a great confidence-booster as you're likely going to receive some lovely compliments from the guys you meet.

Dating can also be demoralizing, as a guy can turn out to be a real jerk. When you go on a date, you are putting yourself out there and allowing yourself to feel vulnerable. You are essentially about to be judged, examined, interviewed and ultimately accepted or rejected.

Remember you are, of course, going to be doing the same to him. You do not need to give up all the power to the other person. Sometimes though, we all feel a bit fragile, and at such times you're more sensitive to being judged. The dating journey is certainly one through unchartered, and at times, hostile territory. There may be times when you'll be tested, pushed and pulled this way and that.

Keep up your resolve. You may feel it's you who's doing something wrong, or you're being 'too picky', or you'll 'never meet the right guy'. There's nothing wrong with kissing a few frogs before you find your prince! It's par for the course. Just as in life, you may not know what's up ahead, but you can choose which road to take. This is when you need to stay focused and keep your eyes on the prize. Just as Tinderella did, make a list of what you want and don't want in a guy, and don't settle for less than you know you deserve.

Remind yourself of your own AWESOME qualities!

If you're feeling a bit emotional and shaky, make a list of the qualities that make you the awesome person you are. These are the traits people love about you, the traits you know deep down say a lot about who you are. You have your list of what you're looking for in a life partner. Your true love has his list, and he is out there searching for you. It's just a numbers game and it may take a while for you two to find each other.

Remember, your sense of self is not tied to one thing, or one person, nor is it dependent on finding a life partner. It is important to focus on the things that give you joy and on experiencing all that life has to offer.

AN INTRODUCTION TO THE LAW OF ATTRACTION

The Law of Attraction is one of the numerous Universal Laws established over five thousand years ago by the ancient Egyptians, Greeks and Indians. These laws were a means to help us understand how the universe works and more importantly, how we—as humans—exist and thrive within our universe. They pre-date the Laws of Science that came much later such as Einstein's Theory of Relativity and Newton's Law of Gravity.

The Law of Attraction is based on the belief we are all pure energy and are 'vibrating' at different frequencies at any given time. These vibrations are influenced by our thoughts and our emotions, which either attract or repel similarly vibrating frequencies emitted by other living things. Put simply, whatever you imagine and think about, you will bring **to** you. Whether it is something you want, and whether it is positive or negative. To take this further, according to the Law of Attraction, you can manifest anything you desire—wealth, optimum health, love, happiness, holidays, houses, cars.

What you think about, you bring about

Growing up, most of us were more likely to be taught we have to work hard to get what we want, and that nothing comes by chance. Yet according to the Law of Attraction, the power to manifest lies within each of us—as long as we are clear about what we want. This is why people use vision boards, motivational quotes and positive affirmations. These help them become clearer on what they want in life, and to strengthen the belief they deserve these good things. This then strengthens the positive vibrations happening within a person and 'attracts' similar positive vibrations in the things and people they want to bring into their life.

Regardless of your beliefs around the Law of Attraction or other metaphysical beliefs, it's important to be clear in who you want to attract in a partner. If you focus your thoughts on pain and anger (negative emotions) you're still feeling about men who've hurt you in the past, then you are likely to continue to attract these qualities in a man because you are still 'emitting' negativity.

If you heal and embrace the learnings from past hurtful experiences and what they have taught you, this will help you become clearer on what you don't want in a guy or in a relationship, as well as the positive qualities you are seeking. This can only help you in your journey as you'll attract the right guys to you and repel the ones who aren't right for you.

AN INTRODUCTION TO ASTROLOGY

Astrology is probably more widely understood and accepted than the Law of Attraction. There aren't many newspapers, news sites or magazines which don't include star signs readings or astrology predictions for the day, week, or month. Astrology is one method different cultures have used for centuries to determine the compatibility of a partner, and the search for love is a primary reason many people read about astrology.

Astrology has a depth that goes beyond the few lines for each star sign in a magazine. It is a field of study based around the movement of the planets and stars, which seeks to explain how humans co-exist and interconnect in our universe. Astrology is truly vast and delves deeply into the planetary movements, including rising signs, ruling planets, houses and more. It is well documented, so it's relatively easy to learn about astrology, whether through traditional avenues or online. Many online sites will offer you individual 'readings' or personalised charts—some are free, but many will charge for these.

Know your star sign

The twelve signs of the Zodiac are fairly well known in today's society as a means to understand and predict behaviours and events in people's lives—whether you believe these interpretations or take them with a grain of salt. Astrology dictates that success in your choice of partner is highly influenced by the compatibility of your star signs.

The Zodiac is made up of four categories, or 'elements': water, fire, wood and air. Each of the twelve zodiac signs belongs to one of those four elements, and each element has different strengths and weaknesses. For example, the water signs of Cancer (which Tinderella is), Scorpio and Pisces are said to be intuitive, emotional and artistic. People who have star signs in the same element or a compatible one are more likely to be well-matched because they understand each other better and have similar character traits. This is likely what Derrick would have meant when he wanted Tinderella to be a Leo.

Some people are more rigid about their belief in this concept than others, and not all so-called 'incompatible' star sign unions result in failure.

BELIEF SYSTEMS CAN HOLD YOU BACK

Astrology and the Law of Attraction are belief systems people can apply to their lives, or not. These belief systems provide interesting insights to ponder or have fun with, or they can be a serious guiding force in people's lives. Any belief system which is rigidly adhered to can create friction with potential partners who don't share the same beliefs, or not to the same extent. These beliefs can be used almost like emotional armour, as in the case of Derrick.

Derrick presents as someone who is extremely rigid in his beliefs—to the point of exclusion and rudeness. It's possible he has been hurt in the past and in seeking to control the pain or reframe the situation in a way that made sense, he may have attributed this to an incompatible star sign union. If that is the case, he will be governed by his unresolved pain and fearful about his choice of future partner being in the 'wrong' star sign, to the point of avoiding women who have an incompatible star sign.

He ended the date and fled from Tinderella as though a crab had bitten him. What a shame he couldn't just enjoy the date and the opportunity to meet someone interesting and fun. Oh well... next!

LEARNINGS FROM TINDERELLA AND DERRICK:

1. Dating is a journey, so it's going to have ups and downs, good times and bad. In the wobbly times, remind yourself of how wonderful you are and the qualities you bring to a loving relationship.

2. Be clear on what you want in a guy because, according to the Law of Attraction, what you think about is what you will attract—whether it's positive or negative. Make sure your *K.I.S.S. List for Mr Right* focuses on the positive traits you are looking for in a guy, rather than a list of the negative qualities you want to dodge. You're more likely to meet guys who have those positive qualities.

3. Astrology and the Law of Attraction are belief systems that people ignore, acknowledge or embrace to varying degrees. If you're open to meeting people in general, you're more likely to enjoy the breadth and depth of different experiences in life. Remember, if you meet a guy who is rigid in his beliefs, then your lives together and your choices in life are likely going to be governed by his strong belief systems. This is great if you share the same belief systems as him, but not so great if you don't.

Chapter 19

Ken

Lovers don't finally meet somewhere. They're in each other all along.

- Mawlana Jalal-al-Din Rumi

Tinderella had culled her chat list. Juggling her real life and online commitments was very time consuming. She was now casually chatting to just a few guys online but was yet to connect with a man worthy of a second date.

Ken was the one who had really held her interest.

He was cheeky and often chatted about sex. This didn't perturb Tinderella at all. She was a big fan of sex and found it was a good way to create a playful conversation with a guy. Such conversations also gave some good insights. Surely if he had several stories of sex, he had to be desirable, and hey—everyone has a history when it comes to dating second time around, don't they?

Judging from his profile picture, Ken was a dreamboat. He was tall, handsome, and a dad of two, so he was well rehearsed in dealing with the needs of a family. He showed patience and understanding for Tinderella's daily challenges. She could talk to him about a multitude of things because he too had a broad range of knowledge and experiences in his life—including two marriages.

Ken's first marriage had been very short. He'd been way too young and didn't understand the responsibility of marriage. The second lasted twelve years and had ended on the spot when he'd found his wife in bed with his brother.

As Tinderella messaged with him in increasingly lengthy conversations, she formed a picture of someone who was a very popular, social character, always surrounded by mates, male and female. He was a man in his prime, and he was well and truly aware of that fact. He had returned to the gym and had a beautiful, strong physique. He wasn't shy in posting pictures, and she could see his muscles bulging through his shirt, and a hint of the many tattoos that covered his body.

Ken indicated he was not looking for a relationship, but he would be accepting if one happened to fall into his lap. It was at night when he felt lonely. Despite his popularity, he was tired of taking a different woman home every night to his bachelor pad. He had been a professional football player, and he had played for most of his adult life. He still loved anything to do with football and typical of a champion, he was shy until he had a couple of drinks, when he became the centre of attention and the life of the party.

Every woman wanted him, that was a given. He was a smooth talker and made every girl he spoke to melt at his feet. He was Mr. Popular and Mr. Sexy all in one.

Tinderella was about to find this out for herself.

She and Ken had agreed to meet up for a date.

He was out with his friends at a club event and wanted to meet her in person. He couldn't get out of the event and asked Tinderella to come and meet him instead.

Why not? she thought. It would be a safe place, and he had said she could bring a friend as he had a few single mates there that night, too.

Tinderella would bring her friend, Jodie, who was also single and a fabulous addition to any party. She was a fellow hair stylist, and a social media influencer within the hairdressing industry. Jodie had an effervescent personality and was able to talk to anyone.

They decided to get ready at Tinderella's house.

Jodie arrived with an armful of clothes and accessories. She squealed gleefully as she came through the door, dropped the clothes to the floor, and gave Tinderella a huge hug of love. They had a very special friendship, and Tinderella was blessed to have Jodie in her life. She was a true soul sister, and they had been through many a rough time together. Although others had tried to test them, and cause a rift between them, it was never possible. They were besties, and nothing was going to change that. She scooped up Jodie's pile of clothes, walked into the bedroom and threw them onto her bed. Jodie followed her and flopped onto the bed, laughing, asking for the details of their night ahead.

Jodie would be playing the role of wing girl, and her job was to look after Tinderella. She hadn't met Ken in person, and needed Jodie's assessment of him, and what his vibe was. Tinderella knew Jodie was the girl for the job.

Jodie jumped up and went into the kitchen, looking for her favourite champagne. It was their pre-going out ritual. A glass or two of champagne at home made dressing up more fun, gave them a chance to catchup, and got them into the mood for going out. When they got together, they could practically talk underwater.

Tinderella was in charge of the music and opted for 80's flashbacks. It was party time!

They decided to go with a disco theme, with a bit of shimmer and sequin glamour. Tinderella chose a sexy black top she had purchased from one of her favourite boutiques, where there was often a jewel hidden amongst the racks. It seemed tonight was the night for its first outing. She matched it with her fitted, black faux-leather pants and sexy gold stilettos. Her hair went high in a messy bun, and she added large gold hoop earrings that had silver teardrops at the base of the hoop. Tinderella was in heaven. She looked like a new age Donna Summer, sexy and sultry in one outfit.

Perfect. She could wear her silver waterhole bracelet, and it would all work together.

Jodie opted for a sexy black dress with a large multi-coloured necklace and chunky dance boots. She looked amazing! Her black hair was down, and it framed her perfect features, highlighting her high cheekbones and luscious, naturally plump lips.

The pair giggled as they sipped champagne and applied their make up for the evening. Jodie expertly applied false eyelashes on Tinderella's eyes, then commanded her to open them—and wow! They looked amazing! Her eyes had become the centrepiece of her face, and they sparkled like jewels in the night. Tinderella had applied a shimmer to her eyelids, completing her look. She was a walking disco! They looked in the mirror, admiring their finished results. They were both beautiful women, unique in their own way, and together they made an attractive addition to any event.

Tinderella moved to the couch to brief Jodie about Ken, showing her pictures of him during his heyday. There were also more current pictures he'd messaged her of him showing his six-pack. She giggled at Jodie's reaction. Tinderella's favourite 80s song played in the background. Terence Trent D'Arby had a very sultry, hip sound and in his time, was pretty hot too! They sang along to the lyrics in between chatting about the evening ahead. They were both very excited. Ken had ordered the girls an Uber to bring them to the club. This was a first for Tinderella and she was very flattered he had considered this for Jodie and herself. The Uber beeped on arrival as per Ken's request. Tinderella took her house key off her key ring and hid the remaining keys under the cushions of her couch. A girl can never be too sure, she thought.

The destination was about fifteen minutes away, and the friends talked and joked the entire way. They could hear the live band playing as they pulled up at the club. It sounded busy. Hearing a Bon Jovi cover pumping through the speakers was certainly a blast from the past. They entered the pub and Tinderella looked around. She couldn't see Ken, so they decided to go and have a drink at the bar. Jodie opted for sparkling wine and Tinderella settled for a nice pinot gris, not the house pinot, something with a bit more vintage.

Tinderella and Jodie chatted happily over the music and were deep in discussion about some new business ideas when Tinderella felt a body press against her, and a voice in her ear.

It was Ken, whispering his hello.

Tinderella turned to find the most delicious man she had ever seen standing before her. She hoped her appreciation wasn't too obvious. Wow! Fucking wow! Ken pulled her into his arms, held her close to him and looked into her eyes. He began to stroke her hair, playing with the wisps that hung loosely around her face. His hand went to her cheek, then to her chin, and he lifted it to look deeper into her eyes.

'You are more beautiful than I could ever hope for,' he said. He kissed her cheek, then the other cheek and then he kissed her full on the mouth.

At that moment, Tinderella swore she heard fireworks, and the butterflies in her stomach had come to life and were fluttering around them both. It was a kiss straight out of the movies she had watched, where romance was born, and passion and lust all came together at once. It felt like the kiss went on forever. Ken pulled her closer, and their bodies moulded together. Uh oh. Tinderella was out of her depth with this one. She felt like Cinderella and Sleeping Beauty in one—she had just been awakened from a coma and here was the guy who was going to be her prince. Ken held her when the kiss finished and swayed with her to the music. Far out, this guy had all the moves, and he knew it.

Was Tinderella ready for this?

Could she keep a level head and not get too hopeful too fast?

She had no idea, but in that moment, everything was perfect. Ken held her close and began to hum softly into her ear.

'So, how are you?' he asked, with a cheeky half smile.

'I'm well,' Tinderella replied, trying not to give too much away.

She was intrigued. How had she met a guy like this on an online site? So, she asked him why he was on the dating sites, and where was his 'Barbie'?

He got the joke and replied his friends were his social life, and he had needed time to repair from his ex-wife's betrayal. He had only recently decided to go online, after his mates had persuaded him to join up. He'd only been on the dating app for a matter of weeks and was neither here nor there with it, but he was happy he had met Tinderella through it.

Oh, he was smooth, she thought.

He then leant in to ask her to go somewhere a little quieter. They went outside, through to the courtyard. It was a beautiful night, and the sky was clear and shining with stars. They found Ken's group of friends and in typical fashion, Jodie was already with them. Ken introduced Tinderella to the group, and they welcomed her with hi-fives, waves and handshakes as they introduced themselves. She felt so easily accepted by the group and commented to him how lovely they all were. He told her that he rarely invited girls to meet his mates, but he knew she was different and would be worth it.

When their drinks needed refreshing, he held her hand as he took her to the bar. He wasn't letting her go, and he was making it known she was his date tonight. She was just having fun in the moment and not thinking too far ahead. She could clearly see he was a potential player and was going to be very hard to peg down. So why try? Tonight was going to be a fun night out. She had her bestie with her, Jodie was having a great time too, and the night was still young.

Ken walked with her back to the group and stood behind her with his body pressed onto hers. The electricity between them was apparent. Tinderella could feel his breath on the back of her neck. Every so often, he would kiss her there in an intimate and discreet way. Tinderella watched his interactions with his friends during the night. They seemed to have a lot of time for him. Many were friends from his years of football and school days. This reassured Tinderella about Ken as a person. She was impressed he had kept such strong connections over the years, despite his turbulent relationships, and was just as impressed by the career Ken had built after his sports success. Many ex-sports people were left without any qualifications to help them succeed in the real world and create financial stability for themselves beyond their glory days. Ken had succeeded at this in spite of his personal hiccups. He now worked as a sports consultant to A grade sporting teams, helping maintain health and wellbeing within their clubs to see them realise their full potential.

He asked Tinderella to dance. The song was medium-paced, perfect for dancing. She was comfortable on the dance floor, but she was still feeling a little blank. Admit it! She was in shock! This guy seemed to be the perfect package.

Was it real?

Was this a fantasy night that would end if her slipper fell off?

Oh Tinderella, stop over-thinking!

And with that, Tinderella decided to enjoy her time with Ken and accept the night for what it was. They walked back into the courtyard, where the night had become a little chilly. Ken moved them over to stand near the outdoor heater and directed her to stand in front of it, whilst he stood behind her and kept her back warm. He turned her to face him so they could talk and asked her more questions about her life and her future. This wasn't something Tinderella was ready for and she was caught a little off guard by the questions.

It seemed Ken was fishing to see whether she had the answers he was looking for.

He explained he was over the dating scene and he was now looking for something a little more consistent. The way they had connected online had left him asking if she was the girl he wanted to spend more time with. It was an open statement, and Tinderella was unsure what to think. Was this real, or was this a well-rehearsed way he used to get women to submit to him?

It was a risk she was willing to take. Successful or not, it would be another life experience she would discover and learn from. Ken and Tinderella rejoined their group inside, but things were different now. She was interested to see where the night would go for her and Ken, without his friends, and Jodie, her gorgeous wing girl. He must have sensed her desire to leave and suggested they return to his place. They could buy a bottle of wine on the way.

Tinderella agreed. She gave Jodie a hug and checked whether she was happy to stay with the group. Jodie agreed to stay and promised to leave her Find Friends app open on her iPhone. Tinderella could track her every movement during the night. Jodie would do the same for her.

After settling on a bottle of Australian pinot gris, they took an Uber to Ken's place. He reached for her and hugged her close to his body. He was very strong and had taken care of himself. He also seemed to be in a good space mentally too, after everything he had been through. She wasn't sure what the night had in store for her or them as a couple, but she was here now, and Ken felt nice sitting next to her in the Uber. They arrived at his address and he held the car door open for her. He had good manners, and he knew how to treat his lady, that was for sure.

Ken's home was a modern, architecturally designed house with all the latest gadgets. He placed the bottle into the fridge to chill and then showed Tinderella around his magnificent home. The kitchen had all SMEG appliances, with digital sound and lighting controls, and beyond it was a beautiful enclosed pool area. It was a house that could have been plucked right out of the next century. She giggled and asked if this was where the Jetsons lived?

He smiled, and after pouring their wine into two long-stemmed glasses, indicated they could sit outside, on the modern outdoor wicker lounge suite. They took their places by the fireplace set into the wall between the inside and outside of the house, warming both zones. The flames were mesmerizing, dancing with the gas that fuelled them.

They sat in the quiet space for a few minutes, until she broke the silence.

'Ken, you have women falling at your feet. Why me?'

He paused for a moment before responding.

'Because you excite me. You intrigue me in every way,' he said.

It was so sweet, the way he responded, and Tinderella felt she had made the right decision in coming to his house with him. There was obviously a connection between the two of them, and she knew he felt it too.

He asked Tinderella to tell him more about herself, so she began to tell him about her past, her marriage and how she had grown in the time she'd been single. She had embraced her life and was now ready to share it with someone.

Ken had an odd look on his face and asked more questions about her marriage.

It seemed as though he was trying to understand what she was saying, and interrupted her again, asking her about the man that had been her husband. Tinderella told him more about her ex, and where the marriage had gone wrong.

Ken asked her ex's name, and Tinderella told him.

He was silent. Tinderella couldn't understand why, and she asked him if he was okay.

He didn't reply immediately, and she was confused, not sure of what he was about to say. Ken was clearly trying to choose his words wisely, and he began slowly, telling her that he wasn't aware she had been married to the same man who was one of his closest friends.

Tinderella was shocked by what he said. This was going to complicate things. Not for herself—for Ken. She had given her ex-husband her past, but she wasn't going to sacrifice a future with the most amazing guy she had ever met in her life for him. But it wasn't only up to her.

Now there were three people sitting on the couch.

Ken was very quiet. It was as if he had put up a wall to protect himself against the backlash of what could be. What if she never had the chance to prove to this man she could be a loyal and loving partner to him, never mind his connection to her ex-husband? Tinderella didn't want to come between the two men, and that made it hard to find the words to convince him otherwise. It had taken her a long time to find Ken, and with all of her heart, she didn't want to lose him. She wanted to grab him and make passionate love to him. It seemed awkward now, almost uncomfortable. Why couldn't they return to the kisses of three hours ago?

She could feel Ken was distant now. He was battling with the decision to continue with her and a potential new relationship, or the potential to lose a friend.

Even though they had never met in person before, and theirs had been a random online introduction, she knew it would be hard to explain to her ex-husband. Would he be angry? A relationship with Ken suddenly seemed further and further from her grasp. There were no words to describe her disappointment.

It was up to Ken who had to decide what he wanted more. A life with Tinderella, when he had already told her she was someone he was looking for. Or the solid bromance he had with her ex. If this was handled correctly, couldn't all parties be happy?

He still had to make the choice.

Ken was so quiet, just staring into his wineglass. Tinderella knew it was a problem that wasn't going to go away overnight. She was sad, and numb. To feel such a connection and then have it snatched away at the last minute was devastating. She quietly asked Ken to call her an Uber.

She hugged him goodbye and climbed into the car. Sitting in the backseat, she replayed her actions and their conversations in her head over and over again. There was nothing she could do. She had tried to protect herself from the pain if something went wrong—and something had. Now Ken was potentially just a memory. She had really hoped he would have been brave enough to take her in his arms and hold her forever.

Tinderella was still numb when she arrived home to her empty house. The silence in the house was eerie, as both children were away with their father for the weekend. She was so sad, she couldn't even cry. She was tearless. She had never felt so helpless to fix a situation.

She walked into the kitchen and poured a glass of spirits from a bottle in her liquor cabinet. She didn't care what it was. She just wanted something to numb the pain. Tinderella was a problem solver, but she was dealing with facts here. She knew that guys had a code. And she had just become bro code collateral.

It was up to Ken.

Tinderella just had to be patient and wait to see if this spectacular man would come to her.

But was she hoping for more?

Was it a fantasy that would never come true?

Tinderella poured herself another shot. She wasn't a big drinker, but tonight was different. Tonight was about masking the pain and numbing her poor heart. It had stopped in its beat the moment she heard of Ken's mateship with her ex. He could be the love of her life or her biggest disappointment.

Tinderella feared she knew the ending; she just didn't want to accept it tonight. She wanted to stay in that place where a little bit of hope still lived, but her head was ruthless.

And she hated her head for knowing.

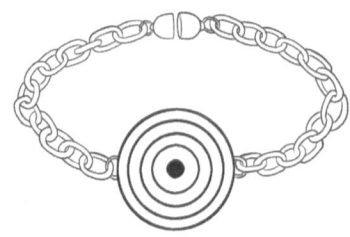

It's Time to Talk... by Simone

DEALING WITH TRUE LOVE, FAIRY TALES AND REALITY

You have embarked on a journey to find a guy who you'd like to ultimately share your life with. The man who will love and accept you unconditionally and help you become the best version of yourself. The man who will be your rock and challenge you when needed but will also be the 'soft place' to fall when you're hurting or feeling vulnerable. These are just some of the common things in many people's descriptions of 'the One'.

The reason why fairy tales and romance movies are so popular is because they appeal to our desire to be loved... To be rescued from ourselves and our lonely lives... To be freed from a life of struggle and uncertainty... To live a life of joy and 'happy ever after'.

However, fairy tales and Hollywood romance stories are not without their own challenges or heartaches—think Snow White nearly dying after eating that poisoned apple, or Cinderella having to escape the clutches of a controlling step-family, or Allie's rich family blocking Noah's attempts to marry her in *The Notebook*. But at the end of the day, love wins over any challenge and the guy and the girl live happily ever after. Or do they?

We can't always rely on a 'prince' to do the work in finding us (although I can assure you—he is looking for you!). We also don't have a fairy godmother to help us with the choices we make in life (although BFFs such as Jodie are a close second!). What we do have is access to the greatest font of knowledge and joy available—that which is found within ourselves. Trust in yourself to make the right choices in life, and even if they aren't the right choices, they will result in experiences abundant in learnings.

AN INTRODUCTION TO THE BRO CODE

Ken could quite possibly be 'the One' for Tinderella, but he needs to make a difficult choice to be with her. That choice would require him to break the universal law between mates—the 'bro code'. And the code's number one rule says *'Thou shalt not look sideways at another man's girl'*.

As Tinderella acknowledged, there are serious consequences if a guy breaks that code, including potentially losing a friendship and likely his other mates as well. It's clear Ken places a high value on the friendships he has with his mates, so he would not make such a choice lightly.

Why do people break the code?

Tinderella and Ken's story represent a situation where they've met and connected, and then realised they had a connection through an ex—the '6 degrees of separation' phenomenon. You can't help who you fall in love with or are attracted to. Sometimes people can be secretly attracted to their friend's ex. If this is acted upon, the resulting liaison can be illicit (in an attempt to avoid losing friendships), or public, and can cause a lot of hurt if not managed respectfully.

Is it possible to break the code and walk away with a friendship intact?

It's a tricky one. In Ken's situation, it comes down to how accepting his mate, Tinderella's ex, is of each other's lives, happiness and choices post their divorce. There are guys out there who could definitely work things out with their mates to be okay with that mate dating an ex. Ken and Tinderella's situation, in which they'd never previously met each other, might make this a little easier.

No doubt, there would be many women who say that this code applies to them, too. After all, women too, have deep friendship ties.

The degree to which a guy would be okay with a mate dating his ex is directly proportionate to where he is in his own healing journey after his breakup. If the pain or anger is still quite raw, then when a guy dates his best mate's ex, this would be felt as a massive violation of the bro code. If, however, the guy has completely moved on from the breakup, and holds no ill feelings, resentment or regret about his ex, then there is a higher chance if his mate wants to date his ex, the guy could be okay with it.

Second to the guy code is honesty. If there's potential for a relationship with a mate's ex, then it's best to be upfront and honest with him and discuss this with his mate, instead of seeing the guy's ex behind his back.

What should the woman do?

In a word—nothing. Tinderella made the right call here. It's best for the guys to sort it out between themselves. Some women may try to coerce or encourage their guy into talking things over with their mate, or even choosing them over their mate, but that's never a good thing because his decision to break the code needs to rest solely with him. This is a decision he will need to make on his own and he will therefore need to be prepared for the consequences (good or bad) of that decision.

If the outcome isn't great, and he loses his mate in his decision to pursue a relationship with his mate's ex, then he is less likely to harbour resentment towards his new girlfriend for the loss of his mate's friendship if she has stayed neutral throughout.

THERE'S MORE TO THE JOURNEY THAN JUST THE DESTINATION,

The intensity of dating and the urgency of finding a life partner can be overwhelming if you let it. Yes, you're probably going to be stood up, let down, rejected and maybe even hurt along the way. You'll also likely meet some guys you'd rather forget. Consider these experiences bumps in the road.

After a date that leaves you a little disheartened, tell yourself that you are one guy closer to meeting 'the One'. Consider every guy you meet who doesn't tick your boxes helps to reinforce that you are honouring your list, which means you are honouring yourself.

Your online dating journey can be loads of fun and it's important you remember to enjoy this time in your life. You'll be meeting new people, going out for coffees, breakfasts, lunches, dinners and parties. You'll hear lots of interesting stories about other people's lives and you'll have the opportunity to share your life stories with others. You might try new activities with your dates, such as bike riding, going on picnics, drawing, art or photography classes. You'll probably see many movies during your dating journey and maybe go to more concerts or events than you've been used to on your own or with your friends.

Sharing your dating journey with girlfriends can make it even more enjoyable. It's not just Maverick who has a wingman in best mate Goose in the movie *Top Gun*. Wing women are just as awesome! How fabulous Tinderella's best friend could join her in getting ready for her date.

As the saying goes, *'What you put into life is what you get out of it'*.

LEARNINGS FROM TINDERELLA AND KEN:

1. Have fun during your dating journey! Share it with a friend. Look for interesting places and events to share with your dates. This can be an exciting and enriching time of your life.

2. Breaking the Bro Code is not something to be taken lightly. You can't help who you fall in love with, but if you fall for your ex's mate, then this is something the mates need to work through themselves with honesty and respect. Similarly, if you fall in love with a best girlfriend's ex, you will need to do the same with her, or risk losing her friendship.

3. And finally, the guy who is 'the One' for you is looking for you, too! Have faith you will find each other and more importantly, enjoy the journey.

The Reflection

The biggest adventure you can take is to live the life of your dreams.

— Oprah Winfrey

It was time for Tinderella to clear her mind and process the events of the past two years. So much had changed in her world since becoming single. The earth was still spinning. Time was moving on at a pace that was leaving her feeling overwhelmed and frustrated. Ideally, she would be able to stop time with a snap of her fingers and catch up to where life was easier to understand.

She had taken the chance to escape from reality for a few days, to the crystal clear beaches of The Whitsundays, one of her favourite places in the world. The moment Tinderella landed here, she felt a sense of peace. It was exactly what she needed. Time away, to re-order her thoughts and map out her future. Her coping mechanisms had been tested, and she needed to take the chance to breathe again.

Her room was the essence of luxury. It was furnished with locally sourced handmade furniture and finished with silk curtains and scented candles. Carved wooden animals and ornamental statues decorated every corner and the huge bed took pride of place in the centre of the room. It had a white silk canopy that hung seductively from the high four-poster frame. The coverlet was a pale pink with complementing throw cushions, ornamental flowers and a welcome pack, placed strategically on the bed. It included an eye mask, scented foot cream, aloe vera gel and Desert Lime Oil - a nourishing serum that could be used on either her hair or her body. It was a beautiful addition to the normal guest pieces most hotels provide.

The open plan room had a beautiful flowing feel and the sliding doors to the bathroom allowed the bath to have a full view of the ocean. The beautiful timber balcony acted like a stage to showcase the bluest of blue ocean. Leaning over the railing, she could see all the tropical fish playing amongst the coral. The coral, the seaweed, the different canals and tunnels that the fish darted in and out of gave the little creatures endless hours of fun.

Tinderella knew she had chosen the right place to stay and rejuvenate her mind and her body.

Holding a cocktail with one hand she opened the bamboo fabric curtain and stepped out onto the balcony. Mother nature, always beautiful and inviting, held out her hand to show the holidaymaker her world. Tinderella could not describe the feeling of peace and how important it was for her to reconnect with her Earth. To reground herself and fill her lungs with the precious air was a release. Exhale the past and embrace the future. Leave the wrongdoings and the mistakes behind and start anew.

Tinderella realised she had learned to love herself during the time of her newfound independence.

Being single didn't mean she had to be alone in her soul. It meant she had choices. It meant she was free now to find the man she wanted in her future life. But until then, she was happy to be patient. She was happy to manifest a magnificent future for herself. She was in her prime and she had come to learn she was a beautiful, desirable woman who had many talents. Tinderella had grown confident in many ways; in her communication, in her actions and in her body. Sexually, she had become a free spirit, and she had finally gained knowledge she'd only dreamed of. And Tinderella was proud of herself.

This was her time.

She had come out of her cocoon and transformed into a beautiful butterfly.

And despite all the bumps along the way, she knew she couldn't stop now. She would embrace life with both hands and an open heart. Tinderella's journey would go on. Smiling, she closed her eyes and let the sun shine down on her like a promise from the Universe.

References & Resources
Become Part of Tinderella's Tribe

THE JOURNEY WITH TINDERELLA CONTINUES...

Join our tribe to feel supported.

Continue Tinderella's journey of learnings and fun in her world of online dating.

- Join our mailing list to receive free resources and the release of our second book.
- We have prepared a number of resources to support you on your journey to find true love, including Tinderella's *K.I.S.S. List for Mr Right*. These are free to download from www.talesoftinderella.com
- Follow us on Facebook: https://www.facebook.com/talesoftinderella/
- Follow us on Instagram: https://www.instagram.com/tales_of_tinderella/
- Follow us on Twitter: https://www.twitter.com/@talestinderella
- Order Tales of Tinderella merchandise at www.talesoftinderella.com/merchandise
- We are happy to start a conversation. Please email us at info@talesoftinderella.com.

COMING SOON:

Podcast Channel:

Subscribe to our Podcast Channel: *Tales of Tinderella with Julie Okely & Simone Hamilton*

One-Day Tinderella Workshop:

The learning doesn't stop with the book!

Register your interest for our informative one-day Tales of Tinderella workshop by visiting www.talesoftinderella.com/workshops.

This includes:
- Your own *K.I.S.S. List for Mr Right*
- An online dating profile that really wows!
- Tips on how to attract 'the One'
- Ideas on how to start and continue great online conversations
- Advice on how to manage difficult dates and avoid guys who are wrong for you

Five-Day Tinderella Retreat:

Empower the single woman in you!

Join us in 2020 at Tinderella's retreat by registering at www.talesoftinderella.com/retreats

Our signature five-day retreat in an exotic location is a truly life-changing experience that will leave you feeling inspired, excited and ready to manifest the life you deserve.

Learn the following over the course of five days:
- Explore who you are and what you want in life
- Clarify your vision for the future
- 'Clear' your blocks that are holding you back in every aspect of your life
- Challenge your beliefs and expectations about relationships and love

- Feel empowered, confident and ready to attract lasting love into your life
- Design the man you want to attract in your *K.I.S.S. List for Mr Right*
- Learn about human behaviour and dating in the modern age
- Enjoy a makeover and style update with guidance from experts in fashion, styling, photography and makeup artistry
- Feel equipped with tools and information to navigate your online dating journey

About the Authors

Julie Okely is a proud Ksmilaroi Indigenous Woman and a successful freelance hairstylist and owner of Dilkara Hair, where she has the opportunity to hear a multitude of stories by dozens of vivacious single women looking for love and adventure.

Julie is a multi-award winner including the Supply Nation Indigenous Business Woman of the Year 2017, as well as a passionate Innovator, Writer, Educator, Manufacturer, TEDx speaker and a Telstra Business Women's ACT Awards finalist.

Julie is a proud mother of two children and lives in Canberra, Australia.

Simone Hamilton is a Behavioural Change Specialist with a successful hypnotherapy and coaching practice. Simone supports her clients in clearing their blocks as well as helping them open new doorways to the amazing possibilities that life can offer.

Simone coaches her peers – hypnotherapists, psychologists and counsellors – in developing their own successful therapy and coaching programs. Simone is also the creator of the Tree Ring Method© – a customised program designed for people to accept, process and rise above challenging issues and events.

Simone is a proud mother of two children and lives in Canberra, Australia.

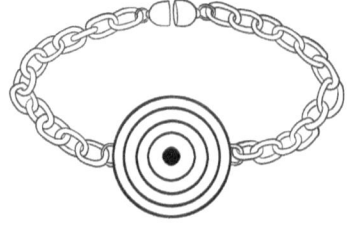